FREE TO SOAR

STEP INTO A LIFE OF FREEDOM AND PURPOSE

JOHN BOWMAN

Free to Soar and *Free to Soar Workbook* are self-published by John Bowman and Your Freedom LLC. All rights reserved. No part of this publication may be reproduced, stored in a retrieval system, or transmitted in any form or by any means—electronic, mechanical, photocopying, recording, or otherwise—without the prior written permission of the publisher, except in the case of brief quotations used in reviews or articles.

ISBN: 9798283248738

Unless otherwise indicated, all Scripture quotations are taken from the *Holy Bible, New International Version®, NIV®*. Copyright ©1973, 1978, 1984, 2011 by Biblica, Inc.™ Used by permission of Zondervan. All rights reserved worldwide. "NIV" and "New International Version" are registered trademarks of Biblica, Inc.™

This publication is intended for educational and inspirational purposes only. It is not intended to serve as a substitute for professional counseling, medical advice, or therapy. If you are experiencing emotional distress or mental health challenges, please seek support from a licensed professional.

Visit: www.freetosoarbook.com

Copyright © 2025 by John Bowman

BOOK ENDORSEMENTS

"As a pastoral counselor and executive performance coach to pro-athletes and CEOs, I've witnessed the profound human longing for healing, hope, and identity. In *Free to Soar*, John Bowman masterfully combines biblical wisdom with psychological insight and actionable guidance, creating a pathway to authentic freedom. Both tender and bold, this book speaks directly to those ready to release the burdens of their past and step into the fullness of their created purpose found in Jesus."

— *Dr. Johnny Parker, Author of Frontstage/Backstage, Former Johns Hopkins Adjunct Professor*

"For the past decade I've seen John in the trenches with those who are overcoming addictions and limiting mindsets. What he shares in this book isn't theory, it is lived wisdom that can transform your life and empower you to change your future."

- *Joël Malm, Author and Leadership Coach*

"In a world where so many are weighed down by shame, regret, and fear, Free to Soar offers a refreshing breath of God's truth and grace. Pastor John Bowman writes with the heart of a shepherd and the strength of a teacher. This book will equip you to rise above your past and walk boldly in the freedom Christ paid for. It's a timely message for the Church and for every believer who knows there's more to their story.

In the past few years as I have grown under the Leadership of Pastor John, I can vouch for every word written is to inspire and change lives. It is my personal recommendation for readers to receive the book as a prophetic declaration of the Lord over your life to be able to step into your true potential and walk into your destiny designed by God."

— *Pastor Anuradha Das, House of Prayer, India, Author of Supernatural Life, Amazon*

"Reading Free to Soar felt like having a heart-to-heart with someone who sees the gold in you, even when you forget it's there. John Bowman writes with such clarity and compassion, calling you back to who you really are in Christ and pulling greatness to the surface. This isn't just a book, it's a breakthrough. If you're ready to rise, heal, and step into the freedom that's already yours, I can't recommend it enough."

— *Harrison Wilder, author, corporate strategist, creator and host, Success Sundays with Harrison*

"Free to Soar is more than a book—it's a journey of transformation. As the leader of the Freedom Mentoring program, I've walked alongside many people longing to break free from what holds them back and step into the fullness of who God created them to be. This book is a powerful companion for that journey.

Each chapter is packed with biblical truth, practical tools, and honest encouragement. Whether you're just beginning to discover your identity in Christ, or you've been walking this road for a while, Free to Soar will meet you where you are and guide you forward—with grace, clarity, and purpose. It's a roadmap to healing, restoration, and lasting freedom—and I can't wait to see how it changes lives."

— *Andrea Shanahan, Freedom Ministry Leader & Freedom Life Coach*

"Free to Soar is a powerful reminder that while the world teaches us to simply survive, God created us to thrive. Through 21 faith-filled chapters, this book offers more than encouragement—it delivers spiritual clarity and direction. Each page will draw you closer to Christ and equip you to rise above fear, doubt, and limitation. If you're ready to move from surviving to soaring in your faith, this book is your lift-off."

— *JJ Moses, Author, Speaker, Former NFL Athlete*

Foreword

BY JOEL OSTEEN

I believe God puts dreams in our hearts not to frustrate us, but to lead us into the life of purpose and abundance He created us for. So often, though, we get stuck — held back by the past, weighed down by fear, or caught in the cycle of self-doubt. That's why I'm excited about this powerful book *Free to Soar* by my friend John Bowman.

John has a heart to help people discover the freedom that is already theirs in Christ. He understands that true transformation doesn't come from behavior modification, but from the inside out—by renewing our minds and aligning our hearts with God's truth. In this book, John walks you through a personal journey of healing, hope, and breakthrough. He doesn't just give you inspiration — he gives you practical tools to help you let go of what's been holding you back so you can step fully into the life God has for you.

Whether you're coming out of a difficult season or stepping into something new, *Free to Soar* will encourage you to rise above your limitations, embrace your identity in Christ, and pursue your destiny with boldness and faith.

My prayer is that as you read these pages, you'll feel God's love drawing you higher, stirring up new vision in your spirit, and reminding you that you were made for more—you were made to soar.

Keep believing, keep growing, and keep pressing forward. Your best days are still in front of you!

Joel Osteen
Senior Pastor, Lakewood Church

ACKNOWLEDGEMENTS

I am deeply grateful to Joel Osteen for his inspiring messages of hope. Without his leadership and encouragement, this book would not have been possible.

Thank you to Dr. Paul Osteen and Pastor Craig Johnson for their vision and for seeing this book within me before I ever could. I'm also thankful for Pastors Steve Austin and Barbara Curtis, who have been both advisors and friends along the way.

To my wife, Laura — thank you for your heart for the hurting. Your support, wisdom, and constant encouragement to "go the extra mile" have helped shape the way we reach people. You make me better, and I am forever grateful for your love and belief in me, faults and all.

Special thanks to Ruby Lopez; Manny and Vanessa Dorado; Patricia Zavala; Karsten Smith; Shayne Simpson; Ndidi Ananaba; Rashaan Listenbee; Andrea Shanahan; Matthew and Emily Linehan; Eric Carroll; Jason Diaz; Kris Durrett III; Tommie Rambo; Glenn and Carla Bone III; Malachi Burden; Carlos Cardona, Bruce Gibbons — and to all the Freedom volunteers, facilitators, leaders, and participants around the world. You've helped shape this program into far more than a curriculum — you've made it a movement.

Thank you to my good friends Erik Luchetta, Derek de la Peña, and Melanie Stiles for being such a meaningful part of my journey to freedom.

This book is truly a team effort. We are more than a team — we are family. The Freedom Family.

Thank you,
John

Table of Contents

Introduction 1

Chapter One
You are Free 7

Chapter Two
Go with the Flow 21

Chapter Three
Perspective is Everything 41

Chapter Four
Know Yourself 55

Chapter Five
No More Limits 69

Chapter Six
Cut Yourself Some Slack 81

Chapter Seven
Change Your Mind 93

Chapter Eight
First Things First 103

Chapter Nine
What are you saying? 115

Chapter Ten
The Game Changer 125

Chapter Eleven
From Prey to Pray 135

Chapter Twelve
Higher Power 155

Chapter Thirteen
An Attitude of Gratitude 173

Chapter Fourteen
Letting Go of the Past 183

Chapter Fifteen
Fly Free 193

Chapter Sixteen
Take the Mask Off 205

Chapter Seventeen
What's Your Story? 217

Chapter Eighteen
No Judgment Zone 227

Chapter Nineteen
Birds of a Feather 239

Chapter Twenty
Living Life on Mission 249

Chapter Twenty-One
The Sniff Test 259

Appendix
WHAT'S NEXT? 282
Discover Your Design 283
Freedom Growth Process Worksheet 288
Memorization Scriptures 292
Freedom Certificate of Completion 299

About the author
John Bowman 303

INTRODUCTION

I love eagles. They glide effortlessly through the sky, exuding strength, confidence, and a sense of purpose. They seem to have it all together, soaring above the world with power and grace.

But they didn't start that way.

In the beginning, eaglets are weak, completely dependent on their parents for food and protection. Their tiny heads wobble unsteadily—so much so that they've earned the nickname "bobbleheads." Their world is small, safe, and comfortable.

Imagine what the young eagle might think: *Why should I leave? Life is good here. It's warm. Food comes to me. I have the perfect view.*

Yet if they stayed in the nest forever, they would never reach their full potential. It's only by leaving – by stretching their wings, facing the unknown, and learning to fly – that they grow strong.

And when they do, they own the sky. They soar effortlessly, riding the wind, reaching speeds of up to 100 miles per hour. They become what they were meant to be.

Your struggle is not the end

Like young eagles, life sometimes pushes us out of comfort into challenge. You may be wondering:

- *Why am I going through this?*
- *When will things get better?*
- *Why does it feel like everything is against me?*

Perhaps you're battling depression, anxiety, addiction, grief, or financial hardship. Maybe you've lost a loved one, gone through a painful divorce, or feel stuck in isolation.

You might even be turning to unhealthy coping mechanisms — alcohol, drugs, or distractions that don't truly heal the pain.

But there is hope!

Trust the process

Reaching your full potential requires trusting the process.

What most programs have discovered is belief in a higher power is critical to your inner freedom. This is the first step in many recovery groups.

I'd like to take it a step further. I believe your freedom comes through Jesus. He is that higher power. If you've tried other programs with limited or no success, I encourage you to try Freedom. It is based on the principle that Jesus came to set you free. You could even say that it's a one step program. Take a step toward Jesus, and He'll change your life!

Freedom is a journey

It doesn't happen overnight. That's why it's called a journey. You will be going through a process to become fully whole.

That takes some time and effort. But as the saying goes, you can pay me now or pay me later. There is a high price for low living. If you want to be totally free from life's struggles and/or addictions, you have to make the decision that you are sick and tired of being sick and tired.

When I was a kid, we didn't have wireless phones. We didn't have Google or Apple Maps. We had to use paper maps that we would unfold and navigate. You couldn't call someone if you were lost.

Worst case, we would stop at a gas station and ask for directions. Many times, that didn't work out so well either.

These days we have a Global Positioning System (GPS) so we know where we are at all times. We can track our progress and know where we are on our journey. For *Your Freedom Journey*, I've created the **Freedom Roadmap** to help you know where you are on the journey to freedom.

It's not about how fast you get to your destination; it truly is about the journey. Healing takes time. Self-discovery takes time. Letting go and forgiving takes time. Don't rush the process. Take it a day at a time and you'll be amazed at how far you go and how much you will change.

We aren't using a Global Positioning System but a God Positioning System. God is much better because He knows the beginning from the end. He created you. You are in good hands.

The real question is,

Are you ready for a change?

If your answer is "Yes", I invite you to join me on your journey to freedom. Along the way, you will find milestones, like mile markers on the highway.

As you progress along the journey and complete the milestones, you will see yourself let go of the past and become everything you were created to be.

What does it mean to be whole?

Integrity means to be whole and undivided. If you get on an airplane and it's got a screw loose, you don't want it to take off. While it can be frustrating for the pilot to share that we have a maintenance issue and can't take off, you don't want them to fly without fixing the problem.

In the same way, some of us have a "screw loose" so to speak and need to "tighten" it to be whole. Maybe it's something that happened in your past. Someone hurt you and did you wrong. It's hard to forgive. Maybe you've isolated yourself trying to gain control of your life, but it only made things worse. Now you feel alone. Whatever your issue is, we want to help you on this journey to freedom so you can fulfill your God given purpose.

After leaving Egypt, the Israelites had to go around a mountain in the desert for forty years.

God said, "You yourselves have seen what I did to Egypt, and how I carried you on eagles' wings and brought you to myself."[1]

---

1. *Exodus 19:4*

But Israel didn't experience their promised land. They could have been living in the land of milk and honey enjoying the good life, but they didn't want to pay the price of doing it afraid. They had a victim mentality. They didn't trust that God would do what He promised. They chose fear over faith and suffered the consequences.

Don't go around the same mountain for the next 10, 20, or 40 years of your life. If you give this process a year of your life, you can experience the fruit of it for the next 39 or more years.

Eagles in scripture

God often uses eagles as a symbol of strength and renewal:

- Moses said: "like an eagle that stirs up its nest and hovers over its young, that spreads its wings to catch them and carries them aloft."[2]
- Isaiah wrote: "but those who hope in the LORD will renew their strength. They will soar on wings like eagles; they will run and not grow weary, they will walk and not be faint."[3]
- David declared: "Praise the LORD, my soul; all my inmost being, praise his holy name. Praise the LORD, my soul, and forget not all his benefits" . . . "who satisfies your desires with good things so that your youth is renewed like the eagle's."[4]

My hope and desire for you is to find inner wholeness and move forward toward your God given destiny to become everything He created you to be. Just keep going whether you feel like it or not. Take it a day at a time.

God's promises are true. He is working all things together for your good and His glory.

---

2. *Deuteronomy 32:11*
3. *Isaiah 40:31*
4. *Psalm 103:1-2, 5*

FREEDOM ROADMAP

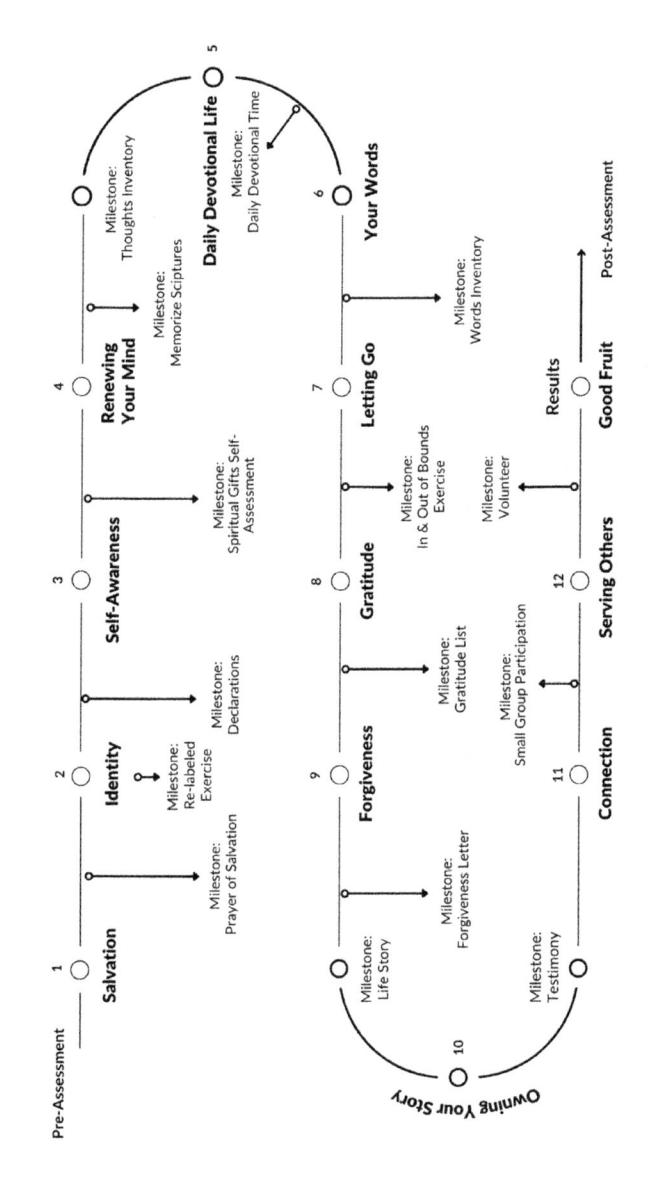

Pre-Assessment

1 Salvation
Milestone: Prayer of Salvation

2 Identity
Milestone: Re-labeled Exercise
Milestone: Declarations

3 Self-Awareness
Milestone: Spiritual Gifts Self-Assessment

4 Renewing Your Mind
Milestone: Memorize Scriptures
Milestone: Thoughts Inventory

5 Daily Devotional Life
Milestone: Daily Devotional Time

6 Your Words
Milestone: Words Inventory

7 Letting Go
Milestone: In & Out of Bounds Exercise

8 Gratitude
Milestone: Gratitude List

9 Forgiveness
Milestone: Forgiveness Letter

10 Owning Your Story
Milestone: Life Story
Milestone: Testimony

11 Connection
Milestone: Small Group Participation

12 Serving Others
Milestone: Volunteer

Results

Good Fruit

Post-Assessment

© 2025 by John Bowman. All Rights Reserved

Free to Soar Pre-Assessment

Unlock Your Potential Today

Scan the QR Code Below

freetosoarbook.com

Chapter One

YOU ARE FREE

For years, we have heard the phrase *"Thank God It's Friday"* – or TGIF. It's a common expression, but have you ever stopped to think about what it really means?

At its core, it reveals a deeper truth: We struggle through the week just to get to the weekend. Life sometimes feels like a burden, something to endure rather than enjoy. We wake up stressed, rush through our days, and count down to a temporary escape. Then we start it all over again on Monday.

But what if we didn't have to live that way?

What if every single day – Monday through Sunday – was filled with joy, peace, and purpose?

The weight we carry

The world teaches us to survive, but God created us to thrive.

So many of us carry invisible burdens. Stress, anxiety, depression, fear, addiction, isolation – each one weighs us down, holding us back from living in the freedom God has for us.

The global pandemic didn't create these struggles, but it certainly exposed them. In the first year of the pandemic alone, the World Health Organization (WHO) reported a 25% rise in anxiety and depression worldwide.

Research from Boston College found that by the end of the pandemic, 50% of adults experienced anxiety, and 44% battled depression – rates six times higher than before.

And the numbers don't lie.

- Teenagers: Mental health struggles skyrocketed. In the UK, the number of teens (16-19) receiving disability benefits for mental health conditions doubled in just a few years.
- Adults: Many turned to unhealthy coping mechanisms—substance abuse, social media distractions, or endless work—to numb the pain.
- Older Adults: Some found renewed purpose, but many suffered from increased loneliness, financial struggles, and declining mental well-being.

Even after the world "returned to normal," the emotional struggles didn't just disappear. The masks came off, but the wounds remained.

Maybe you've felt it too. Maybe you've carried a weight that no one else can see.

How does stress show up in your life?

Is it anger?

Addiction?

Anxiety?

Depression?

Do you find yourself pulling away from people just to avoid the pain? Or maybe you scroll through social media for hours, hoping to escape for a little while?

Sometimes it's more subtle than that.

Maybe you just don't feel satisfied, even when things are "going fine."

Maybe it's that nagging jealousy – of a friend, a co-worker, or someone online.

Or maybe, if you're honest, you've started to rely on control or manipulation to feel safe.

And then there's that quiet ache ... the feeling that you're not where you thought you'd be by now.

Whatever it looks like for you, I want you to know something: **God has more for you.**

- He doesn't want you just getting by – He wants you to live in real freedom
- Freedom from the weight you've been carrying
- Freedom to breathe deep, rest easy, and experience peace that doesn't make sense on paper – but feels like exactly what you have been needing

Freedom in the middle

Many people believe that peace comes when problems go away. But the truth is, storms will come. Jesus even warned us:

> "I have told you these things, so that in me you may have peace. In this world you will have trouble. But take heart! I have overcome the world."
>
> John 16:33

God's promise isn't that we won't face struggles. His promise is that we don't have to be bound by them.

When your identity is in Christ, something shifts. You no longer live for the weekend – you live in the freedom of His presence, every single day.

This doesn't mean life will be perfect. It doesn't mean you'll never feel anxious or stressed. But it does mean that anxiety won't have the final say. It means that even when life feels overwhelming, you can stand firm, knowing that God's peace is greater than any storm.

Your Freedom Journey begins here

So, how do you step into this kind of freedom? How do you break free from stress, fear, and anxiety?

Your Freedom Journey is designed to walk you through that process. In the pages ahead, we will explore how to:

- Identify the strongholds that keep you stuck
- Replace lies with God's truth
- Develop a mindset of peace, no matter your circumstances
- Break free from the patterns that hold you back
- Step into your God-given purpose

This is not just another self-help book. It's an invitation – to a journey of transformation, healing, and true, lasting freedom.

You don't have to wait for Friday to experience joy.

You don't have to wait for your circumstances to change before you find peace.

Freedom is available to you – right now.

Being content

Paul put it this way,

> "I am not saying this because I am in need, for I have learned to be content whatever the circumstances. I know what it is to be in need, and I know what it is to have plenty.

I have learned the secret of being content in any and every situation, whether well fed or hungry, whether living in plenty or in want. I can do all this through him who gives me strength."

Philippians 4:11-13

Put in today's terms, whether you have a job or not, whether you've lost loved ones or not, whether you've been sick or not, whether you've lost money in the stock market or not, you can be content in every situation. Now, I'm not making light of your grief or loss. I'm simply saying that life happens to all of us. We can get to a place where we aren't moved by our circumstances.

But it's not necessarily the way you think. Or maybe it is the way you think . . .

Our behaviors follow our beliefs

Right believing produces right living. What we believe determines the course of our life.

If you believe there is no God, you are going to live life in that way. You are anchored in the belief "it's every man for himself" and "I better look out for me because no-one else will". It's a selfish perspective.

When you are anchored in Christ, you aren't washed up and down with the storms of life. Your hope is in Him. It is anchored.

Whether you believe in God or not doesn't change the fact that there is a God. But you believe what you believe so you live your life that way.

If you believe in extraterrestrial beings, you will see an alien behind every weather balloon.

In seeking to identify what best sets people free from internal struggles, I have learned that your identity is a key to setting you free.

If you don't believe in God, you will try to make it on your own. You'll try to muscle through it so to speak. Why can't I quit smoking, doing drugs, drinking? Why am I depressed, angry all the time, anxious? When we rely on ourselves, that's exactly what we are going to get. You can't force yourself to change. If you could, it would have worked by now. You don't want to destroy your family, your friends, or your future. You want to do good. But that hasn't necessarily worked for you.

The good news is there's a better way

There truly is freedom through Jesus. See, eternal salvation happens in an instant. That means it takes place the moment you believe in your heart that God raised Christ from the dead and confess with your mouth that Jesus is Lord you are saved.

Then it is a process of "becoming" like Jesus. You are being transformed into His likeness. I know that sounds like osmosis, but it is more like the definition of metamorphosis:

Webster's Dictionary says,

"a typically marked and more or less abrupt developmental change in the form or structure of an animal occurring after birth or hatching. Like the *metamorphosis* of caterpillars into butterflies."

God created you on purpose

You are not a mistake. When you surrender your life and ask Jesus to come into your life, He starts to change you. He is going to change you for the better.

Paul said,

> "Being confident of this, that he who began a good work
> in you will carry it on to completion until the day of
> Christ Jesus."
>
> Philippians 1:6

Remember, you are in the process of becoming. Your personal transformation is a key to experiencing true freedom inside and out. Paul also shared, "Do not conform to the pattern of this world, but be transformed by the renewing of your mind. Then you will be able to test and approve what God's will is—his good, pleasing and perfect will."[5]

---

5. *Romans 12:2*

Your Freedom Journey is a process of becoming.

What have you been through?

For me personally, I went through an unexpected divorce. It was hard. It made me anxious. I was embarrassed and humbled. I was lonely. I felt like a failure. I didn't know what to do. Life lost all meaning. But I received some great advice. Take three years and don't date anyone. Give yourself time to heal.

It was difficult, but during that lonely time, I became alright with being alone. I had never really been alone. Throughout my life, I had gone from one relationship to another in an attempt to never have to face myself.

I spent more time in my morning devotional and prayer. I can even remember the moment I felt healed. If I had jumped into another relationship, I wouldn't have learned anything. That time in isolation made me better.

You may not see it now, but one day you will look back and say, I'd go through that again to be the person I have become. Now, I am a better husband, father, pastor and human being. I have more love and compassion for people. God didn't cause the divorce, but He used it to develop me.

God says,

> "And we know that in all things God works for the good of those who love him, who have been called according to his purpose."
>
> Romans 8:28

It may not feel good now, but the promise is that what you went through or what you are currently going through won't be wasted. Your pain may just be the thing that thrusts you into your destiny.

You are a work in progress

The good news is you don't have to go through the process alone. Jesus said He wouldn't leave you as orphans, but he sent the Holy Spirit to teach you all things. Trust the process!

THE GOAL IS FREEDOM THE ANSWER IS JESUS

Our foundational freedom scripture is John 8:36,

"So if the son sets you free, you will be free indeed."

Right before John 8:36 is verse 32, "Then you will know the truth, and the truth will set you free."

The truth Jesus gives us releases us from the bondage of our past, the bondage of our sins, and the bondage of religion.

Do you want more freedom released into your life?

Jesus is speaking these words to those who were not fully free from man's traditions. Truth must be embraced and worked out through the divine process of spiritual maturity. The Greek word for "truth" is *reality*. To embrace the reality of Christ brings more freedom into your life.[6]

Don't give away your freedom

I encourage you to read the letter to the Galatians. It is an amazing letter to believers to combat us from being dragged back into slavery when we have already been set free through Jesus. We just need to receive it.

Galatians 5:1 puts it this way,

---

6. *Bible Gateway Footnote*

"It is for freedom that Christ has set us free. Stand firm, then, and do not let yourselves be burdened again by a yoke of slavery."

You are completely free through Jesus!
Here are some powerful freedom scriptures:

• You were Crucified with Christ	Romans 6:6-7
• You were Freed from Sin	Romans 6:2-3
• Sin no longer has reign over you	Ephesians 2:6
• You are a New Creation	2 Corinthians 5:17
• You are a Child of God	1 John 3:1
• You are partakers in His Divine nature	2 Peter 1:4
• You are One with Christ	Galatians 3:26-28

What sets people free?

During the pursuit of what truly helps set people free, we discovered some common themes we call the Keys to Freedom.

Some of these are based on my experience leading several ministries, reading books and listening to thought leaders, hearing testimonies of freedom, personally walking out life's struggles with people, and conducting best practice breakout sessions with addiction recovery leaders. Most recently, I became certified as a Mental Health Life Coach[7] to verify we were covering all our bases.

All of it is based on the Bible and the fact that Jesus came to set us free! *(Your freedom may have come through another way and that's great. I would love to hear your personal testimony of change.)*

Your Freedom Journey: Keys to Freedom

- Salvation – Accepting Jesus as your Savior
- Identity – Knowing who you are in Christ
- Self-Awareness – Understanding yourself and your giftings

---

7. *American Association of Christian Counselors (AACC)*

- Renewing Your Mind – Transforming your thoughts with truth
- Daily Devotion – Spending time with God
- Your Words – Speaking life over yourself and others
- Letting Go of the Past – Releasing what holds you back
- Gratitude – Shifting your focus
- Forgiveness – Freeing yourself from bitterness
- Owning Your Story – Embracing your testimony
- Connection – Building a supportive community
- Serving Others – Finding purpose in giving back

Discovering a different way

I was asked by church leadership to assess and realign the recovery programs we were using at the time. They didn't seem to "fit" with Joel Osteen's message of hope and that you aren't defined by your past.

One of the challenges with the main program was that when you sat in your small group, you had to identify yourself by your past or present struggle or addiction. Hello, I'm John and I struggle with a thirty-year addiction with sex, drugs and rock-n-roll.

While many recovery and mental health programs focus on behavior modification, we set out on a discovery journey to create something different - a Bible-based, grace-centered program that emphasizes heart transformation through the work of the Holy Spirit.

The origin of a program matters. For example, Alcoholics Anonymous (AA) is a secular program that influenced the development of Celebrate Recovery (CR), which brought a more overtly Christian perspective. I deeply respect the impact both have had in helping countless people find healing.

Still, some individuals struggle to find lasting freedom through these approaches. Our heart was to create an alternative - one that helps people not only heal but fully step into their identity, purpose, and potential in Christ.

Your Freedom Journey was birthed out of the Bible. It leans into the grace and forgiveness provided to us through Jesus. It is not based on behavior modification, but on Holy Spirit–led transformation. I believe it makes a difference and is a game changer for people struggling with inner wholeness.

When we are saved, we are given a new identity. We are now Children of the Most-High God. The old has passed away and all things have become new. We get a fresh start. A new beginning.

Because of Jesus, we are no longer a sinner but a Saint. Our righteousness comes through Jesus and not ourselves.

Your Freedom Journey focuses on the fact that Jesus came to set us totally free, and we have a new identity in Him. I truly believe this is a better way to change your life and not identify with your past.

COEXIST

Have you ever seen those bumper stickers with *COEXIST* on them, where each letter represents a different religion or belief system? The idea sounds great in theory, but in reality, true coexistence requires something many struggle with - agreeing to disagree. Throughout history, we've seen that tensions arise when personal values and beliefs feel threatened. Even the kindest hearts can struggle to simply let things go.

But here's the thing – I don't want you to stop reading just because you come from a different faith background or wrestle with belief in God. Instead, I invite you to take this journey with an open mind.

Consider it an opportunity to see things from a fresh perspective.

If you've tried everything else and it hasn't worked, what if this is the moment to try something different? Maybe – just maybe – it's time to try Jesus.

Let your journey to freedom begin

Your mission, should you choose to accept it, is to commit to this process for one year. Whether you feel like it or not, just keep going.

- Take it one day at a time.
- Trust Jesus.
- Be transformed.

You were made for more. You were made to soar.

THE FREEDOM COMMITMENT

"Give us a year of your life and it will never be the same for the better"

Joel Osteen

*** In addition to going through this book, I encourage you to get plugged into a good Bible-Based Church and attend the weekend services as often as you can. ***

Your Personal Commitment

I, _____, make a personal commitment to give the Freedom Process a full year of my life. In addition, I commit to attend a main church services weekly at:

_____.

(Bible Based Church)

I will continue through each of the Freedom Milestones and commit to completing the process.

I made this commitment on the _____ day of _____, 20____.

Signed: _____

Chapter Two

GO WITH THE FLOW

In 2021, Laura and I went on a leadership excursion to Cusco, Peru with some friends. We had the opportunity to go river rafting on the Urubamba River in the Sacred Valley near Machu Picchu.

Have any of you ever gone river rafting? Imagine for a minute trying to paddle upstream against the flow. How hard would that be? I have paddled upstream, and it is extremely challenging. At times you may be paddling as hard and fast as you could and not going anywhere. You can spend all your energy and wear yourself out.

What's the process?

There are some things that you can't shortcut. In nature, there is a process for giving life, growth and transformation.

Here are three simple examples:

1. **A pregnant woman** goes through the changes in her body for nine months and endures great pain. She gains weight, stretch marks on her skin and great hardship all for that day she will hold a beautiful baby in her arms. The baby takes time to develop. If the baby is born early, it may die or have physical problems. The woman must

trust that each day her baby is growing and developing into the gift of life that will come to her on that special day.
2. **Farmers** understand the process of seed, time, and harvest. They take great care in preparing their fields, planting the seeds in fertile ground and making sure they are watered and cared for. They don't see progress for some time. Month after month they stay faithful to their crops knowing that one day they will reap a harvest.
3. **The caterpillar** slowly moves along the branches enjoying the leaves. One day, it instinctively knows to make a cocoon around its body. It waits inside as the transformation takes place and it emerges a beautiful butterfly soaring through the sky.

In the same way, God has a plan for our lives. His ultimate goal for all believers is that we be transformed into the likeness of His son Jesus. It takes time. We may endure trials, sufferings, and setbacks, but like the pregnant woman, the farmer and the caterpillar, if we will trust the process, we will be transformed.

Joseph had a dream that he would rule over his brothers. His brothers were jealous of him, threw him in a pit and sold him into slavery. In Egypt, he was unjustly imprisoned. But after enduring trial after trial, one day God set him up to be second in command under Pharaoh and positioned him to save his dad and brothers from a deadly famine.

During the years, Joseph never lost hope. He maintained his integrity and persevered. God had brought Joseph to such a place of maturity and complete brokenness that he was able to forgive his brothers and lead humbly. God used him to save his family.

God's ultimate plan for your life is for you to be transformed into a sterling imitation of Jesus Christ.

TRANSFORMATION IS A PROCESS

To help you with the process, God provides a role model (Jesus), a 24/7 advisor (Holy Spirit), an exhaustive but nontechnical document containing the critical plans, operating principles and performance metrics (The Bible) and a support group (The Church).

Like flowing with the river, if you understand there is a process, you can navigate the challenges of life differently.

So how do you change?

Through thousands of surveys, a research group called REVEAL identified four levels of maturity among believers.[8]

Four Levels of Spiritual Maturity:
- Exploring Christ
- Growing in Christ
- Close to Christ
- Christ Centered

The common catalyst for growth at all levels is:

---

8. *Move: What 1,000 Churches Reveal about Spiritual Growth, March 1, 2016 by Greg L. Hawkins and Cally Parkinson*

REFLECTION ON SCRIPTURE

Specifically focusing on Knowing Jesus.

If you had the answer key for a test, would you use it? The most effective way for you to grow to the next level is reflection on scripture. Now that you know the answer, what are you going to do with it?

What is reflection on scripture?

Reflecting on scripture is a contemplative and intentional process. It's more than simply reading the words on a page—it's about engaging your heart, mind, and spirit in a powerful, personal encounter with God.

In these moments, you're not just learning information—you're being spiritually formed. As you reflect, God is:

- Transforming your mind
- Renewing your perspective
- Revealing truth
- Reshaping how you see yourself, others, and the world around you

Scripture reflection invites you to slow down, listen, and respond. It's a sacred space where you allow God's Word to speak directly into your life.

I've heard people say, I want to love like Jesus, or I can't love like Jesus, He was Jesus.

The truth is, if you will trust the process, His primary desire is for you to become more like Him. You can't force yourself to love people more, but as you are transformed into His likeness, you will love people more. The fruit is a natural output of the process. You will reap what you sow!

Intentional or personal growth and discipleship is helping someone get from where they are to becoming more like Christ. The goal is transformation. How we get there is situational. We are all at different places in our journey. We all learn in different ways.

Along this journey we should move to greater degrees of spiritual maturity. You shouldn't be at the same place next year as you are right now.

Your Freedom Journey isn't linear
What we think our journey will look like

What it actually looks like

That journey will look different for each of us. We all have that perfect vision of what it should look like, but it is often filled with twists and turns, ups and downs, hills and valleys.

As you think about your own personal journey – the ups and downs and all arounds - can you see how you learned along the way? The good news for believers is God promises to work everything together for your good. That perspective changes everything.

Since God is a Good Father and wants to develop and change you for the better, He is using the highs and lows in your life to develop your character.

The question that needs to be asked is, what do spiritually mature people – or at least people who are moving toward maturity – look like?

So, what is spiritual maturity?

Very simply, spiritual maturity is growing to the place where you think, judge, and react biblically to every situation.

When it is the rule and not the exception for you to apply the Bible to your life, when you place every area of your life under the lordship of Jesus Christ.

The Bible calls it Christlikeness, because Jesus is intent on making you like Him.

In a research study, Barna identified these essential elements of discipleship from senior pastors and discipleship leaders (*Here are the top 5 listed in order of importance based on the survey*)[9]:

1. Time with God
2. Prayer and Meditation
3. Personal commitment to grow in Christlikeness
4. Attending a local bible-based church
5. A deep love for God

Many of these elements were reflected in the early church:

"They devoted themselves to the apostles' teaching and to fellowship, to the breaking of bread and to prayer."[10]

In studying church history, I came across a group of believers from Germany called The Moravians[11]. Led by Nicolaus Von Zinzendorf (1700-1760) they were part of a renewal movement within the Lutheran Church.

On August 25, 1727, a prayer meeting started that lasted 100 years.

The Moravians were characterized by three outstanding qualities:

---

9. *Barna Group, The State of Discipleship, 2015*
10. *Acts 2:42*
11. *The World's Greatest Revivals, Fred & Sharon Wright, 2007*

1. Their passionate zeal and devotion for Jesus.
2. Their burden for unity of all true believers that transcended all denominational barriers; and
3. Their fervent zeal for foreign missions that took them to all parts of the world.

What does all this mean?

The primary requirement for this journey is that you be born again.

What does it mean to be born again? You must believe that Jesus is the son of God, that He suffered and died on a Cross and that He was raised again. That's the resurrection. This is what Christians call the Good News. Because Jesus died for your sins, you can now have a relationship with God.

Romans 10:9 puts it this way,

> "If you declare with your mouth, "Jesus is Lord," and believe in your heart that God raised him from the dead, you will be saved."

Having believed, you are "born again" or "saved".

Saved simply means that you have been redeemed by God and are eternally His. You can't earn salvation. It is a gift from God. You simply receive it.

Want some more good news?

Because Jesus overcame sin and death and was resurrected, when you become a believer, you become a Child of God and are set free as well.

One day, Jesus will come back, and you will be raised with Him. The goal isn't just to go to heaven when you die. There will be a new heaven and new earth, and you will receive a new glorified body. You may have heard something different, but that's why what you believe is so important.

You are not alone

Salvation begins a "process" of becoming like him. It doesn't happen overnight, but you don't have to go through it alone. Jesus sent the Holy Spirit to dwell with you and teach you all things . . . you have a helper. Jesus said,

"But the Advocate, the Holy Spirit, whom the Father will send in My name, will teach you all things and will remind you of everything I have told you."[12]

Every believer's journey is different, but the end goal is the same:

TO BECOME LIKE JESUS

We won't be exactly like Him (Perfect) until He returns but, in the meantime, we are perpetually in this process of "becoming".

When you are "in Christ", you can be assured that everything, even trials and difficulties, are working together to make you more like Jesus.

Paul said,

"We continually ask God to fill you with the knowledge of his will through all the wisdom and understanding that the Spirit gives, so that you may live a life worthy of the Lord and please him in every way: bearing fruit in every good work, growing in the knowledge of God, being strengthened with all power according to his glorious might so that you may have great endurance and patience."[13]

God's patterns, principles, promises and processes are true

There are some things that you cannot shortcut. In nature, there is a

---

12. *John 14:26*
13. *Colossians 1:9-11*

process for giving life, growth and transformation. I often say to myself and others, "trust the process".

It's not always easy, but if you recognize that no matter what happens, that as a believer, God is going to work it all out. It makes going through something difficult possible (Not necessarily easier).

Instead of wondering why God did this to me or why I am going through it, my perspective is different. I simply ask God; what do you want me to learn or how can I grow so I can avoid going through this over and over again?

The Prodigal Son[14] is a great example of a "Pattern"

Jesus told a powerful story about a man who had two sons. The older one always did what he was told. The younger one wanted his inheritance early and his dad gave it to him.

He took the money and ran off to have a good time.

How many of us have messed up a good thing? Maybe you weren't satisfied with what you had so you were looking for something you didn't have to fill that hole in your heart.

There's a saying that the grass is greener on the other side of the fence. This happens in marriage or a relationship when we aren't satisfied and think we deserve better.

We can get to a point when so much was given to us that we take it for granted. Maybe we start to feel entitled like we deserve it even if we didn't work for it.

It's no surprise that the young man spent all the money and ended up on the streets begging for food. In fact, Jesus said he longed for the food the pigs were eating but no one gave him anything.

Have you ever reached rock bottom? Maybe you are at rock bottom

---

14. *Luke 15:11-32*

right now. This guy had. But the story didn't end there. Sometimes we must lose everything to appreciate what we had.

The young man came to his senses. That's when we reach the point that we stop the wrong thinking. We stop the pity party. We stop blaming everyone else.

It's hard to admit when we are wrong. He started thinking about how good he had it at home and desired to go back with his tail between his legs and be his father's servant.

So, he got up and went home. But the response he received wasn't what he expected. His dad saw him coming and took off running toward him. He lovingly embraced him.

Then he dressed him up and had a party. God is like that too. He loves us so much; He often reacts differently than we expect. The Bible says that all of heaven rejoices when one person accepts Jesus. God goes after the one lost sheep.

But the poor older brother didn't get it. He questioned his father's decision. Why'd you take him back? Why'd you throw him a party? Why? Why? Why? It's easy to become bitter when something seems unfair.

There are always two sides to a coin.

Jesus was using symbolism to speak to the behavior of the religious leaders who had control at that time. The leaders were asking, why would you come for these sinners when we have been loyal all these years? It even says the older brother, just like the religious leaders, became angry. Instead of being thankful for his brother's return he was jealous and selfish.

Ed Cole said, the pattern of the prodigal is: rebellion, ruin, repentance, reconciliation, restoration. Repentance is what moves us from "ruin" to "reconciliation."[15]

The prodigal son finally came to his senses and turned back to his father who quickly restored him.

---

15. *Edwin Louis Cole, Maximized Manhood, 1982*

The good news is you have a Redeemer who wants to restore you. What's a Redeemer? Someone who gives his life in exchange for your freedom. Jesus sacrificed Himself on the cross and paid the price for our sins. He exchanged His life for ours.

Because of that sacrifice, we can now have a relationship with God.

God is full of grace

As you can see by the story of the Prodigal son, God is full of grace.

When we are far off from Him or we rebel and turn away from Him, all we must do is change direction. That is what repentance is: a change of direction. This is one of God's patterns.

He is for you! He loves you! He accepts you! He approves of you! He is proud of you!

Now,

LEAN INTO GOD'S GRACE

The woman at the well[16]

God will go out of His way to save you, heal you, and help you in your time of need.

There was a woman in Samaria who went to the well to get water. Jesus showed up and changed her life. She was living in shame. She had been divorced many times and the man she was living with now wasn't her husband.

Moreover, Jews weren't allowed to associate with Samaritans. They were already considered unclean regardless of everything else she had done.

---

16. John 4:7-30

Jesus knew all this and cared about her anyway.

He had a conversation with her without judging her. He didn't condemn her or throw scripture at her.

She had gone to the well at a time when no one else would go. She was probably avoiding the gossip and looks from other people. Have you ever isolated yourself or avoided people just because you knew they were looking down on you?

Jesus told her everything she had done. She was confronted by her truth, and He accepted her anyway. That's life changing.

Jesus shared how a time was coming when God's worshipers must worship Him in the Spirit and in truth.

His disciples were even surprised He was talking with her. It was probably a scandalous thing to do.

The woman left her water jugs and ran into town to tell everyone about Jesus.

"Come, see a man who told me everything I ever did. Could this be the Messiah?" They came out to see Him for themselves.

See, our life changing experience is so impactful, we want everyone to know about it. We want everyone to receive Him!

As the people were coming from the town, Jesus told his disciples to open their eyes and look at the fields!

Because of the woman's story drawing the people to Jesus, many of the Samaritans from that town believed in Him. He stayed with them two days and because of his words many more became believers.

They said to the woman, "We no longer believe just because of what you said; now we have heard for ourselves, and we know that this man really is the Savior of the world."

The woman caught in act of adultery[17]

What about the woman caught committing adultery? You could get stoned for such a thing. And that's what the religious leaders were hoping for. They wanted to trap Jesus with God's own words.

They already had stones in their hands. But Jesus turned the circumstances back on them by announcing, "If you are sinless, throw the first stone". The truth is, we are all sinners. That's where the saying, "people who live in glass houses don't throw stones" comes from.

Jesus got down on her level. He looked her in the eyes. Do you ever feel unseen? Like people are overlooking you, looking past you when you are talking, or just don't seem to care?

He asked her where are all your accusers? They had all dropped their stones and left. Jesus said, then neither do I condemn you. Go now and leave your life of sin."

That's God's desire for us too. That's repentance. It's turning from our old life of sin and embracing our new life of following Jesus.

Blind Bartimaeus[18]

Do people sometimes try to silence you? They don't want you to have a voice. Maybe they've discounted you and don't even see you.

That's exactly what blind Bartimeus faced. He wanted to be healed. He was excited when he heard Jesus was coming to town. He had heard all the stories about the miracles He'd performed.

Could He heal me too? I'm not going to be quiet. I'm not going to miss my miracle!

He began to shout, "Jesus, Son of David, have mercy on me!"

Shhhh. People firmly told him to be quiet, but he shouted even more, "Son of David, have mercy on me!"

---

17. *John 8:1-11*
18. *Mark 10:46-52*

Don't let anyone get in the way of your freedom! What do you need Jesus to do for you today?

Jesus anointed by sinful woman[19]

Have you ever had someone disrespect you? They think they are better than you?

Do they look down on others? You can tell they don't really care about you. You can't really trust their motives.

Well, you are in good company. Jesus experienced that too. This religious guy had Jesus over for dinner.

A prostitute came and put anointing oil on Jesus' feet. Her tears were dropping onto His feet as she wiped His feet with her hair. This was expensive oil. He then turns to the religious guy and says, basically says, who is more thankful, the person forgiven a lot or a little. The man had not offered anything to Jesus, but this woman gave everything she had for him. He forgave her sins.

Jesus shares with the religious man a story about two people who owe money. One owed a little and the other a great amount. They were both forgiven but who do you think was more thankful?

> "Therefore, I tell you, her many sins have been forgiven—as her great love has shown. But whoever has been forgiven little loves little."
>
> Luke 7:47

Have you messed up a lot? Do you feel like you have so much to be forgiven for? I have some good news for you. Jesus paid the price for your freedom. It doesn't matter if it was a lot or a little. If you've been forgiven a lot, that means you are going to have more gratitude for what Jesus did for you.

---

19. *Luke 7:36-50*

Now that's worth celebrating!

Jesus eats with sinners[20]

If you have life all figured out, you don't really need anyone's help. But if you are sick, you need a doctor.

Back in Jesus day, tax collectors were considered the worst of sinners. They were Jews, helping the Roman oppressors to take money from their own people. And taxes were heavy.

Jesus creates another scandal by eating at a tax collectors house. The religious leaders asked why He would associate with sinners.

That's when Jesus shared that He came for sinners. He came for you and for me!

Which story can you most relate to? Why?

God's principles

Because God's principles are true, they may show up in some form or another in other religions.

The Golden Rule

Did you know the Golden Rule shows up in every major religion (Buddhism, Hinduism, Islam, Judaism)?

> "So in everything, do to others what you would have them do to you, for this sums up the Law and the Prophets."
>
> Matthew 7:12

We should all treat people the way we would want to be treated. That sums it all up.

---

20. *Luke 5:27-31*

You will reap what you sow

You sow seeds every day. When you sow good seeds, you will reap a good harvest. When you sow bad or negative seeds, you will reap a bad or negative consequence.

The Bible says, a good tree can't bear bad fruit, and a bad tree can't bear good fruit.

"Do not be deceived: God cannot be mocked. A man reaps what he sows. Whoever sows to please their flesh, from the flesh will reap destruction; whoever sows to please the Spirit, from the Spirit will reap eternal life. Let us not become weary in doing good, for at the proper time we will reap a harvest if we do not give up."[21]

Death and life are in the power of the tongue

You are either blessing or cursing your future. Your words matter and what comes out of your mouth will frame your life. God spoke the world into existence with His words. We either bless or curse our world with our words.

"The tongue has the power of life and death, and those who love it will eat its fruit."[22]

Give and it will be given unto you

Being generous is a principle. If you give or bless others, you will receive blessings in return. It's important not to do it for that reason, but with the right motives, you can't help but receive blessings in return.

> "Give and it will be given to you. A good measure, pressed down, shaken together and running over, will be poured into your lap. For with the measure you use, it will be measured to you."
>
> Luke 6:38

---

21. Galatians 6:7-9
22. Proverbs 18:21

Have you ever said, "what comes around goes around"? Karma is based on this principle of cause and effect. Most times there are consequences for our actions both good and bad. Karma is simply not based on Christian faith.

There are so many people believing different things that are based on little "t" truths but not the Big "T" Truth of the gospel. Big "T" Truths are based on the Bible while little "t" truths are based on other things. The reason little "t" truths tend to happen is they have a connection to a big "T" Truth.

I recently drove a homeless man to a recovery center about an hour away from Houston which gave us time to talk. He said, the universe is going to help me. I said, that's great. But you know what's greater? The Creator of the Universe loves you and is going to help you.

Why is it so much easier for people to believe in energy or the universe rather than a Creator God who made everything?

The big bang theory

I believe science and theology can coexist. You know why? Because God created science.

I like to tell people that I believe in the big bang theory. That usually catches their attention. I'll follow up with, God spoke the world into existence, and "BANG", it was created.

God's promises

As a believer, God has made certain promises.

All God's promises are "Yes" and "Amen" for you through Christ Jesus[23] is a good one to stand on.

How can you access His promises?

God's Word is His Will. If He said it, He will do it. One way to access

---

23. *1 Corinthians 1:20*

His promises is to pray His word. He is not required to do what you say, but He will do what He promised.

Find where your situation is in scripture and turn God's word into a prayer.

Remind God of His promises.

Pray God's Word

Praying God's Word will change your world.

God isn't obligated to do what you say, but he is faithful to fulfill what He said in his Word. Remember, all his promises are yes and amen. When you pray His promises, He is faithful to perform it. He says, your words will not return to you void.

Whatever you are going through, find where it is written in scripture, memorize it, and put it into action in your life. Like God spoke the world into existence, you can speak life to your world.

For instance, if you are struggling with fear, go to 2 Timothy 1:7,

> "For the Spirit God gave us does not make us timid, but gives us power, love and self-discipline."

What you focus on grows bigger. How big is your God versus your problem? As you focus on God and not your problem, you reframe your life.

Back to the process

As I shared earlier, Joseph went through a process to be positioned to rescue his family from a future famine. It wasn't fair, he didn't deserve what he went through, but those years of trials prepared him and set him up for the future.

His dream came true, it just didn't happen the way he thought it would.

Maybe your dreams haven't happened the way you thought they would. Trust the process. There is a reason for everything. Nothing is wasted.

Like Joseph, what looks like a setback is a set up for your future. You are being developed. You are being prepared. Just keep moving forward.

Remember to go with the flow

So, if God's patterns, principles, promises and processes are true, let's work with them and not against them. Remember to go with the flow. When you are going with the flow of the Holy Spirit, things fall into place. When you resist it, you may not feel peace.

Here's what we know.

- When you become a believer, you become a Child of God
- As His Child, He wants to grow you to become more like His son Jesus
- He works everything including trials to your good. He will use circumstances to grow you
- He has already won the victory over sin and death
- As we become more like Jesus, we start to act like Him
- The result is we display more of the Fruit of the Spirit

The **Freedom Milestones** provide guideposts as you progress on your journey to freedom. Like a map or GPS, they serve to help you know where you are in the process.

The river might be smooth for a while, but you will also experience rapids. There are certain things you can't shortcut or avoid. This process will take time but give it a full year and see how different you can become. Remember to take it a day at a time and if you slip or fall, just get back up and keep going.

Freedom Milestones:

- Prayer of Salvation / Rededication
- Re-labeled Exercise
- Daily Declarations
- Spiritual Gifts Self-Assessment

- Thoughts Inventory
- Memorize Scriptures
- Words Inventory
- Daily Devotional Time
- Make a Gratitude List
- In and Out of Bounds Exercise
- Forgiveness Letter
- Life Story
- Testimony
- Connection: Small Group Participation
- Serving Others: Volunteering

Continue to challenge your perspective. Seek to learn and grow. You can grow with the flow.

As you follow God's process and put these patterns, principles, and promises into practice, you will be changed from the inside out. Trust the process.

Over time, you will go with the flow of the Holy Spirit which will be displayed by the way you act differently to situations. Like a mature eagle, you will fly above the storms of life and have a peace that surpasses all understanding.

Chapter Three

PERSPECTIVE IS EVERYTHING

What's your worldview? Or in other words, how do you see your world?

How we view the world will determine how we respond to others.

If you were born as a white male in northern America, you are going to view the world in a different way than a male born in Saudi Arabia or a woman from India.

What we are taught as children by our parents, teachers, peers and religious leaders all shape our world view. Now we also have social media influencing us.

As well intentioned as these important people in our lives might be, they still come at things from their own perspective. What if they aren't correct? You may go your whole life pushing a belief on others or judging others based on something that isn't true.

I learned that women in the Dominican Republic are judged by having curly hair. They straighten their hair because if they don't, people will treat them poorly. Some restaurants will not serve people with curly hair. This has been a cultural issue of trying to deny the African influence in their country. It may seem silly to those of us who didn't grow up in that culture but for the people who live there it has become a reality. Is there any reason to judge someone because they have curly hair? Absolutely not. But we judge people all the time who are different from us.

As we become whole, our biases should fade away. If we hold on to these biases, we can hurt people and even find ways through the Bible to justify our actions. You cannot judge someone unfairly and be obedient to Christ's teachings. It just doesn't work. Paul said,

"There is neither Jew nor Gentile, neither slave nor free, nor is there male and female, for you are all one in Christ Jesus."[24]

Gaining the right perspective

To develop a healthy and God-centered perspective, consider these key principles:

- **Be teachable** – Stay open to learning and growing in wisdom.
- **Be open to honest feedback** – Invite constructive input from trusted voices.
- **Challenge assumptions** – Question long-held beliefs to ensure they align with truth.
- **Confront personal biases** – Recognize and address any preconceived notions that may cloud your understanding.
- **See the world from someone else's viewpoint** – Practice empathy and seek to understand different perspectives.

Be teachable

I find people are either teachable or they are not. This can also be a form of pride. If you think you know it all or can't learn something from someone else, then you aren't teachable. I take the perspective that I don't know everything and need to seek to understand before reacting to situations.

If you assume you may be wrong and want to learn from others, then you are going to make better decisions.

When considering mentoring or developing someone, I will usually give them something to do or test them in some way to see how they respond. I find that unteachable people aren't going to change and will waste our time. If someone isn't teachable, then you will be frustrated and even do things for them that they should do themselves. This is enabling. In the long run, it just doesn't work.

---

24. *Galatians 3:28*

The fact that you are reading this is a good indication that you are teachable. The true test will be if you put it into practice.

I can't do it for you. You must own your growth. Like the adage says, you can lead a horse to water but you can't make him drink. I can guide you and encourage you, but you must do the work.

Be open to honest feedback

How well do you respond when people give you feedback? Are you defensive?

Do you seek out feedback? When you are open to honest feedback for your improvement, you can grow exponentially.

That doesn't mean you accept all feedback. Some people are simply critical. They criticize everything and everybody. You need to have people you trust and give them permission to give you the feedback you need to hear.

Blind spots happen when we aren't aware of certain negative behaviors we exhibit. I don't know about you, but I want to know how I am coming across to others.

A while back, I was experiencing a great amount of pain in my leg. On a scale of one to ten, it was around a nine. I ended up needing a hip replacement. One day, I asked my assistant if I was acting any different. I didn't want my pain level to change the way I behaved. She said you wouldn't even know you were going through anything. That confirmed what I thought but I wanted that feedback to make sure.

Another time my wife gave me some feedback. We had gone out to eat and I wiped my mouth with my hands. That drives her crazy. She handed me a napkin. At first, I didn't like her giving me that feedback but later I said thank you. I need to be aware of what I am doing. My wife has permission to give me feedback.

Who do you trust in your life who you can give permission to give you feedback?

Challenge assumptions

What do you assume is true? It could be all kinds of things. At one time, people thought the world was flat and that if you went to the edge, you would fall off. We of course now know this isn't true. Assumption is the lowest form of knowledge.

Racism is created largely because it is taught by others close to us usually at an early age. People who are different from us are "suspect". We tend to fear what we don't understand.

When you sit down with someone from a different race, you soon learn that we just aren't that different. Being open to challenging our assumptions is the true test of whether you are teachable or not.

Take a position that you don't know everything. Be open to learn about and from other cultures. John Gray says, "If you don't like people of other cultures, you're going to be very disappointed with heaven."[25]

Do you know someone who is into conspiracy theories? I know someone who researches the end of times. She now believes the world is flat, that we've never been to the moon and many other theories. She says she researches everything but the thing about searches and the internet is the algorithms feed your assumptions. The more you research a topic, the more information supporting your bias will pop up on your device.

My wife and I were talking about a vacation the other day and next thing you know, every ad on our phones was about vacations.

My son is now an attorney. He was taught to argue both sides of an argument. Why? If you can't see an issue from all sides, you will make assumptions that aren't true. You will lose your case because you missed an important piece of the other side's argument.

---

25. *John Gray, Senior Pastor, Love Story Church*

Confront personal biases

An important bias for us to explore before venturing into your personal development is theological bias. What have you been taught about being in good standing with God?

How you answer this will determine your approach toward scripture. The lens we see scripture through needs to be based on truth. We've seen so many people led astray by wrong teaching or wrong viewpoints or a general misunderstanding of scripture.

Occasionally, someone will message me on social media trying to "save me" from Joel Osteen. When I ask if they've ever actually been to a service in person, the answer is always no. I have drawn a line in the sand that I will be happy to hear you out, but you must come to Lakewood with me one time. That will usually shut people down and they will block me after that.

I had one woman take me up on it. She was a student at a bible college in Houston and her professor talked badly about Joel's theology. That Sunday, we sat in the second row. As the worship went on, I looked over and she was weeping in tears. The Holy Spirit was already working on her. When Pastor Joel shared his message, it was powerful and backed up by numerous scriptures.

After the service, she told me she would never let anyone talk negatively about him again. She ended up becoming a member of Lakewood and teaching one of our classes. She then met her now husband there. It's amazing where God will take you if you're not closed minded.

Don't take other people's words or even what you see on video posts about someone at face value. You need to check it out for yourself.

N.T. Wright said, "People often get upset when you teach them what is in the Bible rather than what they presume is in the Bible."

Empathy as a superpower

When you live in absolutes, you miss so much of the world. Why do we box ourselves into what we believe? Usually, it's fear based. We are afraid of what we don't know so we try to find absolutes to give us more control and comfort. The problem is when something doesn't fit in our little box, we seek to disprove it. We close off our minds to ideas that don't fit our beliefs.

We can fall into the trap of thinking in absolutes or black-and-white terms, which makes it harder to see beyond our own narrow view. What would the world look like if we all made a conscious effort to step into someone else's shoes more often?

One of my favorite superheroes is Superman. Superman was strong, could fly, and he fought against evil. His one weakness was kryptonite. It came from his own planet and made him weak and defenseless.

What's your kryptonite?

To me, empathy is a superpower. Jesus is now my hero. I love how He would get down on people's level and see them personally. I think back to the story of the woman at the well.

Jesus met her where she was. He knew her intimately and was able to understand why she acted the way she did. He understood why she hid and came to the watering hole during the heat of the day.

Empathy is a powerful way for us to change our perspective. It can't be done without getting out of your comfort zone (box) and talking to someone different from you. Let me add in one more piece to this superpower. Listening. You can't empathize with someone without actively listening to them and asking curiosity questions to see their side of things.

No judgment zone

I've heard it said, we judge others by what they do and ourselves by our intentions.

What do I mean?

Your wife asks you to do the dishes. You've been watching television all day and don't get around to it. Later in the day she gets upset because the dishes aren't done yet. You get defensive and say, but I was going to do them.

Then you start arguing because you both think you are right.

We tend to judge others by external observation and attributing it to an internal heart condition. Only God can see our heart.

I will frequently tell men not to make any more promises to their wives. You've promised her too many times that you'd change and then don't, so you've taught her not to trust you.

I encourage them to change first, then she will see that you are different. Be the change you want her to see.

There are some denominations who want you to have a visible display of repentance. If you don't cry or react dramatically, you must not mean it. The truth is we all react differently. We are looking for heart change from the inside out.

Everybody has been through something. It's hard not to make snap judgments about people. But here's the thing,

- God loves you and He loves others
- He died for you, and He died for them
- He created you in His image and them too
- He accepts you just the way you are, and He accepts them also

I know it's not easy, but let's create a no judgment zone where we can accept and love each other just the way we are and let God change us and them.

Here's the "I See You" Empathy Challenge:

1. Self-Reflection
Start by recognizing your own perspective. What are your beliefs, biases, and assumptions about a particular topic or situation? Write them down to create a baseline.

_____

_____

2. Identify the Other Perspective
Think of someone who might have a very different viewpoint. This could be someone from a different culture, profession, or background, or simply someone with an opposite opinion to yours on a certain issue.

_____

_____

3. Research or Engage
To truly understand the other perspective, gather information. This could be through reading, listening to others, or even engaging in a conversation with someone who holds a different view.

_____

_____

4. Empathy Exercise
Imagine you are that person. What experiences might have shaped their perspective? What emotional triggers might they have? Try to empathize with their situation, not just understand it logically, but feel it emotionally.

_____

_____

5. Analyze & Compare

Once you've considered their viewpoint, compare it to your own. Are there elements of truth you hadn't considered? Are there areas where your perspective might be limited or biased? Recognize where both perspectives overlap or diverge.

_____

_____

6. Shift Your View

If your exploration has shifted your understanding, be open to adapting your viewpoint. Change doesn't happen overnight, but making small adjustments over time can lead to deeper growth.

_____

_____

7. Action

Lastly, put your new perspective into action. How does it affect the way you approach people or situations going forward? This could mean being more open in conversations, making decisions based on new insights, or simply being more patient with differing viewpoints.

_____

_____

My trip to London

The first time I flew to London it was a life changing experience for me. As we crossed the Atlantic Ocean, I felt a barrier break.

While in London, I started reading the *Financial Times*. The news was so different from what was being reported in the United States. It wasn't based on the American perspective. After that I started seeking out opportunities to travel to different parts of the world. Soon after I went to India, Africa, Croatia, Peru and Australia.

Each time I traveled, I sought to understand the local customs, tried new foods, and shifted my perspective. When we open ourselves up to new perspectives and allow ourselves to learn from others, we start to see things in a different way. The day I realized I didn't know everything was the day I was open to grow.

Mind the Gap

In London, they have an iconic phrase called, "Mind the Gap". The purpose was to protect people from subway accidents by paying attention to the space between the platform and the train. As the train reaches each stop, an automated voice says, "Mind the gap". It's also written with yellow lines at the edge of the platform.

I use this term when developing people to describe the space between where they are now and where they want to be. When we are aware of the gap and intentional with how to close the gap, we can be effective in moving in the right direction.

What's your gap?

Maybe your gap is the distance between you and God. Maybe you are already saved and it's the gap between where you are and knowing Him better. Or maybe your gap is experiencing anger and anxiety and not knowing how to change to have peace. Whatever your gap is, through Jesus, you can experience true freedom.

Defining that gap helps you to know what to do next.

The good news is that God has created a "bridge" for you to get to Him. That bridge is Jesus.

How do you see God?

Do you see God as good? Is He for you? Do you think he will make you sick if you do something wrong?

Do you see God as a Good Father or as someone far off waiting to punish you?

Your image of God will determine your relationship with Him. Many times, our relationship with our earthly father impacts how we see God. If our dad was harsh and didn't show us affection or tell us he loved us and was proud of us, we may see God in a similar way.

If something happened to you that wasn't fair, you may think God doesn't care about you or isn't for you. You might have asked questions like God, why did you allow this to happen to me?

Maybe someone was religious and hurt you, so you quit going to church. God didn't come to give you religion, He came to give you a relationship with Him. Don't let a person chase you from your destiny.

You might also have a wrong perspective of God. For instance, you may think that if you do something wrong, he is going to harm you or make you sick. It's true that we live in a fallen world and that bad things happen. That sickness didn't come from God, and it wasn't punishment for something you did or didn't do.

Jesus said,

> "The thief comes only to steal and kill and destroy; I have come that they may have life and have it to the full."[26]

When my parents got married, they tried to have children. They were later told they couldn't because my mom had severe endometriosis. They adopted my sister Robi who has special needs. They were attending a church but found out that people were making fun of my sister. I wasn't born yet but that is the reason I didn't grow up going to church. After fifteen years of marriage, I surprised them and then five years later my brother came into the world.

Never let people chase you from your dream or your church. I ended up going to church with whoever my girlfriend was at the time. I've been Catholic, Baptist, Methodist, Presbyterian, and Pentecostal. I finally found Jesus at the age of 35 but that foundation could have been laid much earlier. Don't get me wrong, I believe everything worked out and God made up for lost time. My point is, people will fail you, but God will never fail you. Don't put your faith in men, put your faith in God.

God gives us free will. That includes accepting Him. He won't force you. But like the prodigal son, He is ready to run to you. No matter what you have done, He will forgive you. You don't have to clean yourself up first. He is waiting for you.

Everyone knows John 3:16. It is a great declaration of how much God loves you. "For God so loved the world (You) he gave his only son (Jesus) that you wouldn't perish but have eternal life". The good news is that God didn't send Jesus to condemn you but to set you free.

---

26. *John 10:10*

SALVATION IS A KEY TO FREEDOM

I am going to ask you to take a step of faith. Since Jesus came to set you free on the inside, I am going to ask you to take a moment to surrender your life to him and pray a prayer to receive God's grace.

This is the foundation of your journey and will help you gain the right perspective.

You will never be completely whole on the inside until you accept this gift from your Heavenly Father.

Are you ready to receive?

Whether or not this is your first time to pray this prayer or if you are rededicating yourself to Him, I am asking you to say this prayer with me.

PRAYER OF SALVATION OR REDEDICATION
The First Key to Freedom

Pray this out loud:

Lord Jesus. I repent of my sins. I confess with my mouth that you Jesus are Lord and believe in my heart that God You raised Christ from the dead. Thank you that I am saved and Jesus you are now my Lord and Savior.

Date Prayed: _____

[Read Romans 10:9]

Note:

If you prayed this prayer, we believe you are Born Again. That means you are saved for eternity and are now a Child of the Most-High God. We believe and declare that God is directing your steps, and your best days are in front of you in Jesus' name.

We are praying for you on your journey to freedom.

When you become a believer, you receive the Holy Spirit. You don't have to go through the journey alone. The Holy Spirit is transforming you into the image of Jesus. The fruit you will experience is love, joy, peace, forbearance, kindness, goodness, faithfulness, gentleness and self-control.

This is a result of focusing on Jesus.

Chapter Four

KNOW YOURSELF

God created you on purpose and for a purpose.
We all have different gifts, talents and abilities. You are one in now over eight billion people. There is no one in the world like you — never has been and never will be. You are unique.

When you show up or don't show up it matters. The world is better with you in it. We are better together!

Two sides of the same coin

Self-awareness is about having a clear understanding of yourself.

SELF-AWARENESS IS A KEY TO FREEDOM

On the one side, when we understand ourselves better, we can maximize our God given talents and become everything God created us to be. You can also understand where you might struggle and have better awareness of your weaknesses, flaws and limitations.

On the other side, we can better understand how other people see the world. As we better understand our uniqueness, we can better empathize with them and bring out the best in them. We can relate to them and create better connections.

When we assume everyone sees the world the way we do, we limit them and can make wrong judgments about their motives.

I see you

As "I see you", I can help set you up for success. We all want to be seen. As we get to know ourselves and our God given gifts, talents and abilities, we can understand what we are good at and what we are not.

No one can be good at everything. As you run your race in your lane, you can and will be more effective.

One time, I was asked to go to Zambia to help the hospital staff at Mukinge Mission Hospital to know themselves better and leverage their strengths.

During one of the sessions, I was sitting at a large table with about ten nurses and managers. When I asked them what they loved to do, that they were good at doing, the room sat silent. I learned that in their culture, you couldn't say what you are good at because it was considered prideful. After I gave them permission to share and that it was ok, they opened up. One hospital employee shared how she loved to organize the files and make sure everything was in order. I said that is so not me, but I am glad you love it. Knowing what she loved to do, can you see how you could help her do more of that? What would drain me, fuels her.

When you run your race in your lane, you are engaged. You are excited to do it. You excel and do it better than anyone else.

The ideal versus the real

The difference between the ideal and the real is the level of disappointment we will have in life. We have in our mind the ideal spouse, the ideal job, the ideal friend, and even the ideal life.

When our ideal doesn't match up with the reality of the situation, we can become frustrated.

Ed Cole[27] shared a story about a man courting his future bride. He opens the door for her, buys her flowers and talks sweetly to her.

---

27. *Edwin Louis Cole, Maximized Manhood, 1982*

Then after they get married, he gets in the car, reaches across to the passenger side to open the door and then says to his wife, get in.

That's the point when her ideal husband meets the reality of her now husband.

Knowing yourself means being honest with who you are. It's about looking in the mirror and choosing not to pretend to be something you're not.

It's about confronting the brutal facts about us and letting God turn us into the person He created us to be.

That's the ideal.

Run your race

Apostle Paul said,

> "Do you not know that in a race all the runners run, but only one receives the prize? Run in such a way as to take the prize."
>
> 1 Corinthians 9:24

As we seek to know each other, we can leverage each other's strengths and help each other do more of what they're good at. That's how the body of Christ should function.

How's your EQ?

Emotional Intelligence or "EQ" is the capacity to be aware of, control, and express one's emotions, and to handle interpersonal relationships judiciously and empathetically.

Have you ever asked yourself, what's it like to be on the other side of me?

Some people don't care. They may say things like, that's just the way I am, or I don't care what people think about me.

The truth is people with good emotional intelligence have better relationships and tend to be happier.

Personal story

When I was young, we used to ask what kind of mood my dad was in, so we knew what to expect when we got home.

He was a great dad, and I am thankful for all he did to care for us but he was driven by his emotions. If he had a bad day at work, he would take it out on us.

I decided I wasn't going to be that way with my kids. We can't always influence how other people treat us. But we can control how we respond to them in return.

Daniel Goleman's breakdown of Emotional Intelligence (EQ)[28] is so powerful because it shows that managing our emotions isn't just about *feeling* – it's about *responding* wisely.

Quick breakdown of the 5 components:

1. **Self-Awareness** – Recognizing your emotions in the moment
   - Can you name what you're feeling?
   - Why are you reacting this way?
   - The better you understand your emotions; the more control you have over them.
2. **Self-Regulation** – Managing your emotions instead of letting them control you
   - Do you need to react immediately, or can you pause?
   - Not every situation requires a response.
   - Developing self-control means learning to pause before reacting.
3. **Motivation** – Understanding why you do what you do

---

28. *Daniel Goleman, Emotional Intelligence: Why It Can Matter More Than IQ, 2005*

- Are your actions driven by love, purpose, and integrity?
- Or are you manipulating to get what you want?
- A win-win mindset creates better healthier relationships.
4. **Empathy** – Putting yourself in someone else's shoes
   - Can you appreciate other people's perspectives, even when they differ from yours?
   - Empathy builds trust and deepens relationships.
5. **Social Skills** – Creating meaningful connections
   - Strong relationships are key to personal and professional success.
   - Fear of disconnection can hold us back from being vulnerable.

Key takeaway

Emotional intelligence is a skill that can be developed! The more self-aware and intentional you become, the better you'll navigate relationships, stress, and challenges.

Which of these five areas do you feel strongest in? Which one do you want to improve?

Your personal journey

To help you on your journey, let's look at where you currently are and where you want to get to.

What steps can you take now to head in that direction? Honest feedback and direction from trustworthy fellow believers is extremely beneficial to this process.

Who can you include or ask to help you on your journey?

Learning and growing for a believer is a lifelong process. You never really arrive but we can be intentional as we seek to grow.

Here are some ways we can assess, develop and apply what we are learning.

The Freedom Growth Process

1. Assessment

Where are you in your Christian journey? What's your maturity level?

Are you exploring Christ, growing in Christ, close to Christ or Christ centered?

How do others view you?

There are many different assessments you can take to help you know yourself better.

Over the years, I've used assessments like StrengthsFinder, DISC, Enneagram, The Five Love Languages, and the Spiritual Gifts Assessment.

I like to keep things simple so let's start with the *Spiritual Gifts Self-Assessment.*

God has created you with certain gifts, talents and abilities. He is not going to wire you one way and not give you a gift that aligns with how He created you.

For instance, my good friend Erik's number one strength is Learner. Learners make good teachers. When they are learning, they think about stories and how they can best share information with others. It's not a surprise then that one of his top spiritual gifts is Teaching.

Erik is a great Bible teacher who frequently teaches for Lakewood's Monday Night Bible Study. He loves to study the Bible and can share it simply with others so they can understand.

2. Have a growth plan

Determine where you want to go and take steps to get there. If you don't have a plan you are planning to fail.

We all grow in different ways. We also have different learning styles. I personally learn by doing (Kinesthetic). I seek opportunities to participate in what I want to learn more about.

Others learn by reading and writing, verbally or linguistically, still others visually by watching or observing others, and others logically. Some people like groups and others like to learn alone. Find what works best for you.

3. Develop/Apply

Start taking steps and applying what you are learning. You may need to take it a day at a time but start applying what you are learning

Now, thinking about your growth plan, what can you do to develop and grow in this area? At first it might be taking a class or joining a Bible study.

You might find prescribed challenges that will help you grow. I've had several people over the years who wanted to be more comfortable speaking in front of others. One of the things I would tell our interns was to just say "yes" to opportunities even if they scare you. Do it afraid.

I told Vanessa, one of our interns at the time, that I wanted her to teach an upcoming Freedom message on a Friday Night. Even though her facial expression looked scared, she said "yes". She did an amazing job. As she continued to share messages, she kept getting better. She developed more confidence. Sometimes we have to do it afraid.

4. Feedback

Ask for feedback on how you are doing and adjust as needed. As you connect in community, there is a natural accountability. The key is to keep coming. Give someone permission to check on you to see how you are doing. Keep adjusting your efforts as needed.

Proverbs 27:19 says, "as water reflects the face, so one's life reflects the heart."

5. Progress

Have you progressed? How do you know?

As you change, people should notice the fruit of your life change. Then, repeat the process as you grow. You shouldn't be at the same place as you were last year. And next year, you shouldn't be where you are right now.

As you progress, you will also begin developing others.

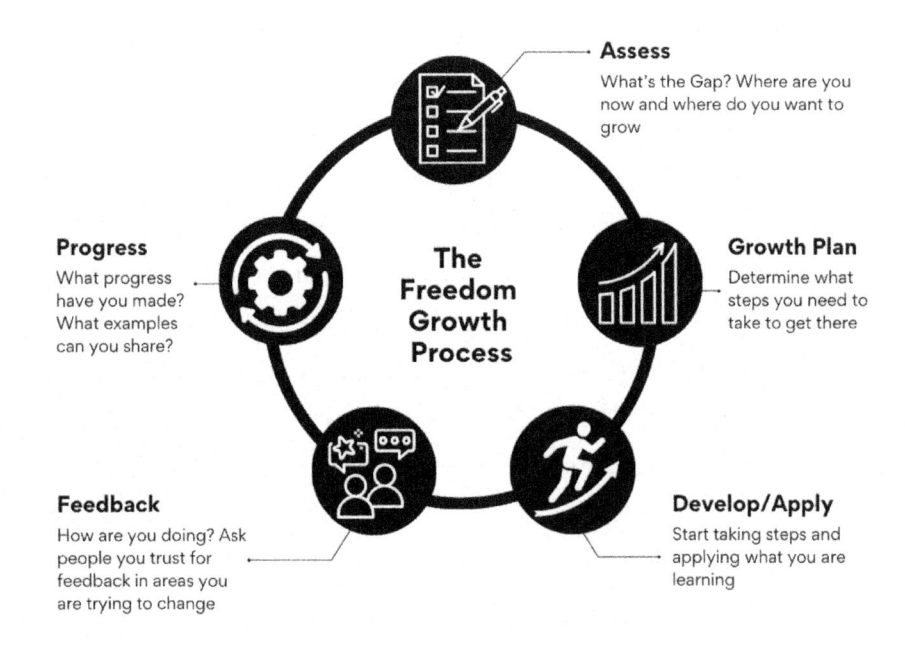

The Freedom Growth Process

- **Assess** — What's the Gap? Where are you now and where do you want to grow
- **Growth Plan** — Determine what steps you need to take to get there
- **Develop/Apply** — Start taking steps and applying what you are learning
- **Feedback** — How are you doing? Ask people you trust for feedback in areas you are trying to change
- **Progress** — What progress have you made? What examples can you share?

Growth Opportunities

You probably haven't heard someone say they are a problem creator but that's what I am. What do I mean? As I am developing someone, I look for opportunities to grow them. Maybe they've never had the opportunity to stretch themselves or lead at a higher level.

Take some time to think about where you want to grow. What can you do to develop yourself. It may be to try something new.

Growth happens when we are challenged. It may be uncomfortable at first but that's the point.

Prescribed challenges

What tasks, projects or assignments can you do that will stretch you where you need to grow? If you are developing someone, the challenge is to determine what would be the best assignment to give someone.

As a leader, I have found that I'm not just a problem solver. I am also a problem or situation creator. I want to identify opportunities to help you grow in the right direction.

When people come to me with a suggestion or say, we should do this or that, I will say things like, why don't you do that and let me know how it goes or develop a plan and let's discuss how you are going to approach it.

Trials

It is difficult to anticipate what trials we will personally go through on our journey (divorce, death of spouse or child, loss of job, disease). These traumatic events can cause major unplanned development in our character.

> "God is more interested in your character than your comfort. He wants you to grow spiritually and become more like Jesus."
>
> Rick Warren

The good news is when you are in Christ everything is working together for your good. Again, trust the process of "becoming".

I would always take my high-capacity leaders on mission trips. It can be easy to have everything together at church when we are doing the same thing week after week. There may not be as many opportunities to see people outside of their comfort zone.

The thing about mission trips is that even though we plan and put everything in order, something unexpected inevitably happens. How do you handle things when they don't go as planned? Can you pivot? Are you flexible? Do you think of solutions to the problem or freeze?

Mission Trips are great development opportunities.

From selfish to unselfish

When you become a new creation, there is a "dying" component. Those selfish desires you used to have start surfacing and you must decide to let them go. When you die to your flesh, your motives and priorities shift. Ultimately, you will be more satisfied.

> "So I say, walk by the Spirit, and you will not gratify the desires of the flesh. For the flesh desires what is contrary to the Spirit, and the Spirit what is contrary to the flesh. They are in conflict with each other, so that you are not to do whatever you want."
>
> Galatians 5:16-17

People often struggle with being content or satisfied. They are trying to fill a God shaped hole with material or superficial things that won't bring contentment. This shift is meant to bring you to a place of contentment where you are satisfied regardless of your situation.

Accountability/Community

We all need help and support. God designed us to be in community.

Who is going to give you feedback on your improvement or be real with you when you aren't improving?

Show me who your friends are, and I'll tell you what you will be like in 5 years.

Seek out the right people who will help and support you on this journey.

Repeat/Multiply

We are a work in progress, so as we grow and develop, we need to repeat the process and reassess where we are and where we need to go and grow next.

As we mature, we need to start doing this same process with others. Who are you developing? God is a God of multiplication. You may not be ready to grow someone else yet, but over time, you will start encouraging others the same way right now others are encouraging you.

Measurement: Lead versus Lag Indicators

In business, there are points of reference called lead and lag indicators. Lead indicators are the things you do on the front end to drive certain results. For instance, if you want to increase sales, a lead indicator might be making more calls per day. The lag indicator would be more sales or more revenue for the company.

Many people try to force lag indicators when it is challenging to maintain them. You can't force yourself to love people more, but as you begin to change, a natural output is you will love people more.

Focus on the *lead indicators* and the results will come.

Measurement
Lead and Lag Indicators

Lead Indicators		Lag Indicators
Salvation	Gratitude	Worshipping God
Identity	Letting Go	Knowing Jesus
Self-Awareness: Know Yourself	Forgiveness	The Word of God as a Lifestyle
Transformation	Owning Your Story	Display of Unconditional Love
Watch your words	Testimony	Fruit of the Spirit
Devotional Life	Connection	Hard to Offend
	Serving Others	Stewardship
		Community

As a Christian, if the goal is to be more like Jesus, what lead indicators should you focus on? You can never go wrong with knowing Jesus better. You might attend a Bible Study or read the Bible every morning.

Here are two foundational keys to make the most of your growth journey: Be self-feeders and ask the right questions.

Be self-feeders:

As you are growing, you need to be a self-feeder. You need to learn how to "feed yourself" and not rely totally on the church for your spiritual growth.

Spiritual growth doesn't happen best by becoming dependent on elaborate programs but through the spiritual practices of prayer, bible reading, and relationships.

Ask the right questions:

What are the right questions? Ask "what" or "how" not "why" or "when". For example, if you are struggling with having the resources you need, the wrong question is why won't they give me what I need or when will they help me?

The right questions would be how can I make the most of what I've got or what can I do to develop myself? Notice the questions take you to being in a position of control. You are no longer a victim but a victor.

I do the same thing when I go through a difficult time. I'll ask, God, what do you want me to learn or change through this trial? I don't want to keep going around the mountain for forty years when I could be living in my promised land today.

As you know yourself and how God designed you, you will be more effective. Now keep going and the growth will happen.

Chapter Five

NO MORE LIMITS

When my son was in middle school, he played football. At one of the games, there was this guy on the other team twice his size. When the play started, he threw my son back six feet. Just hammered him. My son got up and started yelling daddy daddy I can only see out of one eye. I kept repeating, "it's ok son". He kept screaming over and over, "Daddy, Daddy. I can only see out of one eye." I said "come here son. Your helmet got knocked sideways and you're looking through the ear hole".

That's what life is like sometimes. We limit ourselves looking out the ear hole and don't see the full picture.

There is one thing that I do every single day that can change your life. If you get nothing more out of this book, then to remember this - it was totally worth it!

Do you want to know what that is?

I get up every morning and the first thing I say is,

IT'S GOING TO BE A GREAT DAY!

Say that with me. It's going to be a great day.

When my children were young, I would always say this is the day the lord has made, I will rejoice and be glad in it. One day at church, Joel Osteen shared this scripture. My daughter turned to me and said, that's our scripture. I said, it's ok honey. He can borrow it. I'll let you borrow it too.

You might ask, how do you know it's going to be a great day? Well, that's a great question. No matter what happens today, rain or shine, I've set the tone for my day. I've shifted my attitude. I've positioned myself to have a great day.

That doesn't mean everything goes perfect but I'm ready for the day. No matter what life throws at me, I'm ready.

Instead of dragging myself into work or school, I'm excited about what I might experience that day.

Positive mindset

That mindset changes everything. You need to keep a positive attitude. Be hard to offend and quick to forgive. Don't hold on to the negative things people say or do.

When I was in middle school, I was bullied. I know that's hard to believe since I look so tough, but I was small for my age. This guy would hold me down and try to make me say negative things about myself. I held on to this hate for him inside me for years. I would daydream about getting him back. I even worked out and grew stronger just to be ready. I had to release it and let it go before I could move on.

I don't receive that

Several years ago, my nephew shared how his grandfather would constantly say things like "you'll always be sick" or "you'll never be well". He was frustrated. I told him what I'm telling you. Next time he says something negative, say, "I don't receive that". It took a little time but after a while his grandfather quit saying those things. You don't have to receive everything people say to you.

There are things in our control and things out of our control. We can't control how someone treats us or the words they say, but we can control how we respond to it. What have you taken to heart that someone has said to you or about you? What have you said about yourself?

God created you on purpose and for a purpose. Don't let what other people say about you or to you limit you from achieving your goals. You were created to fly.

The lid

There was an experiment done with fleas. The fleas were placed in a jar. They could easily jump out of the jar.

But a lid was placed on the jar for three days. The fleas would run into this lid repeatedly. Then the lid was taken off. Even with the lid off, the fleas would only jump as high as the limit that had been set by the lid.

When they had babies, these new fleas followed their parents' example and only jumped as high as the lid.

What have you put a lid on in your life?

We have a powerful responsibility to help take the limits off ourselves, our children, and the people around us so we can all go further.

Catch your family and friends doing something well. What I mean by that is to be their number one fan. Don't be a lid.

What's a lid? I'm not saying any of you are lids, but if you say things like you'll never amount to anything or you're good for nothing, you're putting a lid on their lives. Instead, tell them you're proud of them. Let them know they are going to do great things.

When my son was young, he was obsessed with sports. He still is today. I told him to find what he was good at, that he loved to do and find ways to do more of that thing.

He went on to get a degree in sports management from the University of Texas.

School came easy for my son. Maybe it comes easy for some of you. My daughter on the other hand had to work at it. Some of you can probably relate to that. I know I can. He didn't study and would still make good grades. It wasn't fair but it was her reality. She made up her mind and pushed herself. She studied extra hard, graduated from college, and today she has a great job doing what she loves to do.

Don't let anything get in the way of fulfilling your dreams. Believe it or not, I was once in middle school. I haven't met a person yet who avoided getting old. Don't look back with regrets. Make the most of today!

There is always a price to pay. You can either pay the price now while you're young, work hard, and do well in school. Or you can play around and later in life have not accomplished your dreams. At the end of the day, the choice is yours. Let's make good choices.

You may be older and feel like it's too late for you. Can I tell you; God can make up for lost time. I wasn't saved until I was thirty-five but here I am twenty-five years later, a pastor serving God and impacting people's lives.

Attitude is everything

My good friend J.J. is only 5'6". People told him he didn't stand a chance of playing football in the NFL. Most of the players are well over 6' tall.

This made him work harder than anyone else. He was fast and determined. He went on to play for the Houston Texans and live his dream.

George Washington Carver was born a slave. But he never had a slave mentality. He strived to go to school even though it was ten miles away back when they didn't have cars. He graduated college. Became a professor. As a scientist he found over 300 uses for a peanut. A peanut! Mr. Carver lived a no-limit life.

My wife, Laura, is from Venezuela. She came to the US over twenty years ago by herself. It was hard but she became a teacher. Years later she bought her own house, met and married me, and is now helping other immigrants coming from her country. She had a made-up mind. She was going to make it no matter what came against her.

Limiting beliefs

Limiting beliefs are thoughts we've allowed into our minds that limit our potential. Maybe someone told you that you would never amount to anything. You're no good. You're a failure.

Sometimes, these beliefs come from fear. Fear is a natural response. If we are being chased by a lion, our fight or flight instincts kick in and we run for safety. Fortunately, most of us don't have to worry about lions.

There are physical and emotional fears. Many of us struggle with emotional fears like the fear of being rejected, fear of failure or the fear of loss.

Do your thoughts tell you:
- I'm not good enough
- I'm too old or too young
- I don't have enough time
- I'm not smart enough
- I don't have enough experience
- I'll never be successful
- I don't have enough money
- I'll never be one of the best
- I'm not talented enough
- I'll never be a great leader

Maybe they stemmed from something someone said about you growing up or something you told yourself and took it to heart.

We must release what people have said or done to us if we ever truly want to be free.

These words play repeatedly in your mind. They limit you from believing that you can do more, that you can be successful. Maybe the dreams you once had are sitting dormant or seem dead.

> "If you realized how powerful your thoughts are, you would never think a negative thought."[29]
>
> Dr. Caroline Leaf

---

29. *Dr. Caroline Leaf, Switch on your Brain, 2007*

Can I tell you that God wants to revive your dreams? He wants you to grab hold of your identity and achieve your dreams.

And maybe you've made mistakes in your past. You are not your past. Your mistakes don't define you. God defines you. You were fearfully and wonderfully made. You may have failed, but you are not a failure. You may have struggled with drugs or alcohol, but you are not an addict.

Let today be the day you let go of those negative labels from your past and put on what God says about you!

Here's another challenge: Be talent scouts

What's a talent scout? It's usually a person whose job it is to search for talented athletes or entertainers.

Do you know that you have talent in your own house?

It's our job to discover our child's talents and foster them. Focus on what they are good at. Do the same thing with your spouse, family and friends. We have enough people against us. Let's not be against ourselves and our own families.

What's your dream?

What are you passionate about? Don't let anything or anyone get in the way of pursuing your goals.

Take the limits off. Be the first in your family to graduate from college, to own a house, to be an astronaut. The sky's no longer the limit.

You only get one chance at this life. Let's take the limits off. I believe in you. Believe in yourself! Dream Big!

You are a new creation!

> "Therefore, if anyone is in Christ, the new creation has come: The old has gone, the new is here."[30]

---

30. 2 Corinthian 5:17

God is re-labeling you. Now, take the old labels off and start speaking the new labels over your life.

Write down some of the labels people have said about you or you've said about yourself.

Now write down what God says about you.

RE-LABELED EXERCISE

Old Labels: **New Labels:**

_____   _____

_____   _____

_____   _____

_____   _____

_____   _____

_____   _____

_____   _____

RE-LABELED EXAMPLES

Old Labels	New Labels
Failure	More than a conqueror (Romans 8:37)
Rejected	Accepted in the Beloved (Ephesians 1:6)
Broken	Made whole (Isaiah 53:5)
Anxious	Filled with peace (Philippians 4:7)
Unloved	Deeply loved (Romans 8:38–39)
Hopeless	Full of hope (Jeremiah 29:11)
Addict	Free indeed (John 8:36)
Weak	Strong in the Lord (Ephesians 6:10)
Shameful	No condemnation (Romans 8:1)
Alone	Never alone (Hebrews 13:5)
Not good enough	Wonderfully made (Psalm 139:14)
Looser	Chosen (Colossians 3:12)
Sinner	Forgiven (Ephesians 1:7)

Declarations

As part of your journey to freedom, I want to encourage you to start declaring what God says about you. As you make these positive statements about yourself, it will reframe your identity.

As a believer, you are a Child of God. God loves you and desires good things for you. That may be hard to believe right now but as you declare what God says about you; it's going to change your:

- Identity
- Perspective
- Mind

- Words

And it's going to build up your self-esteem and encourage you.

Instead of thinking negative things about yourself, you are going to see yourself differently - the way God sees you.

Freedom challenge

- Start making Declaration Statements about yourself each day to start changing how you see yourself.
- Re-label yourself. Write down the old labels of what people called you and then write down the new labels of what God says about you.

DAILY DECLARATIONS[31]
"Say it like you mean it"

I AM BLESSED
PROSPEROUS
REDEEMED
FORGIVEN
HEALTHY
WHOLE
TALENTED
CREATIVE
CONFIDENT SECURE
DISCIPLINED
FOCUSED
PREPARED
QUALIFIED
MOTIVATED
VALUABLE
FREE
DETERMINED EQUIPPED
EMPOWERED
ANOINTED
ACCEPTED AND APPROVED
NOT AVERAGE
NOT MEDIOCRE

I AM A CHILD OF THE MOST-HIGH GOD
I WILL BECOME ALL I WAS CREATED TO BE
IN JESUS NAME! AMEN

---

31. *Copyright © 2021 by Joel Osteen. Used with Permission. All Rights Reserved.*

Chapter Six

CUT YOURSELF SOME SLACK

Are you too hard on yourself? Maybe it's time for you to cut yourself some slack.

That's what God did for us through Jesus Christ. God knows we aren't perfect. The only perfect person ever is Jesus. That's what the cross is all about. God was basically saying, I know they aren't perfect. I know they are going to mess up, but I love them anyway. I want to have a relationship with them so much that I'm going to make another way.

Jesus forgave you. Now, maybe it's time you forgave yourself.

Grace means "Underserved Favor". You didn't earn it. You don't deserve it. Your salvation is a free gift from God. Now cut yourself some slack and just receive it.

I know people who beat themselves up. They are their harshest critics. They think the worst about themselves. They live defeated lives. That's not what God intended for you. He didn't make a mistake. He says, "you are fearfully and wonderfully made." You are a masterpiece.

Paul said,

> "Here is a trustworthy saying that deserves full acceptance: Christ Jesus came into the world to save sinners – of whom I am the worst."
>
> 1 Timothy 1:15

The author of most of the New Testament said he was the worst sinner.

"Even though I was once a blasphemer and a persecutor and a violent man, I was shown mercy because I acted in ignorance and unbelief. The grace of our lord was poured out on me abundantly, along with the faith and love that are in Christ Jesus."[32] The saying "Cut yourself some slack" means to allow one more latitude or freedom than usual, to be more lenient with someone. Sometimes it's easier to cut others some slack but not ourselves. You might say, they just lost a loved one or they are grieving, let's cut them some slack.

In nautical terms, the saying give me some slack is hundreds of years old. Tying a ship to a pier was no easy feat and took two teams of men armed with mooring lines. As one line was pulled to haul the ship the other line was released or "given slack". The process would go on until the ship was properly aligned with the dock.

After we accept Jesus as our Lord and Savior, we receive a Helper, the Holy Spirit. The Holy Spirit's job is to help align us with the image of Jesus.

A work in progress

As I mentioned already, you are a work in progress. We are in the process of "becoming" like Jesus. We won't be perfect until Jesus comes back. That's called the resurrection.

When that happens, you and I will be transformed or changed in an instant and made perfect. In the meantime, give yourself some slack. You are in the process of becoming. You are already free, redeemed, forgiven, and loved.

Why don't you receive God's love and start living like it? You are a victor and not a victim.

You may say, well John, you don't know what I've done. I've messed up too many times. I've pushed my family members away. I've hurt them too many times.

You are not what you've done or what you've been through, you are a

---

32. *1 Timothy 13-14*

Child of the Most-High God. Your trauma is not your identity, and your coping mechanism doesn't define you.

YOUR IDENTITY IS A KEY TO FREEDOM

Listen to what Paul said, "What a wretched man am I! Who will rescue me from this body that is subject to death?

Thanks be to God, who delivers me through Jesus Christ our Lord. So then, I myself am a slave to God's law, but in my sinful nature a slave to the law of sin. Therefore, there is no condemnation for those who are in Christ Jesus." Because through Christ Jesus the law of the spirit who gives life has set you free from the law of sin and death."[33] Paul goes on to say, "Those who live according to the flesh have their minds set on what the flesh desires; but those who live according to the spirit have their minds set on what the spirit desires". See we have to "set" our minds. We have a choice on what we think about. Are we going to be led by the spirit or by the flesh?

The term "flesh," in a biblical context, often refers to the sinful nature of humanity - the part of us that is inclined toward selfishness, temptation, and desires that are contrary to God's will. It represents the human tendency to prioritize worldly pleasures, self-interest, and temporary gratification over spiritual growth and obedience to God.

Now it's time to pick yourself up, shake off the past, and start living in victory.

---

33. *Romans 7*

Big Tom's story

My friend, Thomas, is a gentle giant. He looks like Goliath but has a heart like David. We call him "Big Tom".

I watched for years as Big Tom struggled to maintain his sobriety. He would faithfully attend Celebrate Recovery. He had gone through Alcoholics Anonymous. He would religiously follow the steps, but he never looked free. Life was like a rollercoaster ride.

During the pandemic, things got worse for Big Tom. We launched Your Freedom Journey online but when we were able to, we brought it back into the church. The first time I saw Big Tom; he was a mess. I was so happy to see him! I embraced him.

What I love about **Your Freedom Journey** is that its grace based. It's not by our own personal strength but through Jesus who came to set us free. I told Big Tom to just keep coming.

Remember the lead and lag indicators? Sobriety is a lag indicator. When Big Tom tried to force his sobriety and count the days it led to shame. When he messed up, he was reluctant to come back. You can try to force your sobriety, but it is still based on your efforts. As Big Tom embraced his freedom and cut himself some slack, he began to change.

Over time, I saw the heaviness lift from Big Tom. He smiled. He seemed lighter, freer. What made the difference? Grace.

Big Tom cut himself some slack, leaning on God and not his own understanding, and receiving God's healing power through the Holy Spirit. That's why **Your Freedom Journey** is so effective. Its genesis wasn't in a secular program and a set of rules. Its genesis is in Jesus from beginning to end.

Man down

I never liked the saying, "Man Up!" Back in 2011 when I was asked to take over the church's men's ministry, the guys had shirts with this saying on them. I didn't want to make them stop wearing the shirts so I let it slide but I would frequently reinforce that we can't do it in our own strength. It's not man up, it's Jesus up, and man down.

When we try to do it in our own strength, it is hard. Jesus said, my yoke is easy, and my burden is light.

And I know why they were saying it. There is an issue with men being passive and not taking responsibility in their homes. But I felt like it was sending the wrong message. If we could have forced it or done it on our own, we wouldn't need Jesus, and we would have already done it.

That's why I always say, the goal is freedom, the answer is Jesus!

Now cut yourself some slack. Keep adjusting. Take a deep breath. You are doing better than you think you are. Just keep going. Take it a step at a time, one breath at a time, one day at a time, even one thought at a time.

Why I don't teach the ten commandments

When Moses came down from the mountain after spending time with God, his face shined brightly, and it scared the people. They asked Moses to put a veil over his face.

The Israelites knew the ten commandments but couldn't live up to them in their own strength.

Apostle Paul said through Jesus that veil has been taken away. But more than that, we have the Holy Spirit changing us. As we see Jesus, we are transformed into His image. That's why Jesus came to set us free.

> "But their minds were made dull, for to this day the same veil remains when the old covenant is read. It has not been removed, because only in Christ is it taken away. Even to this day when Moses is read, a veil covers their hearts. But whenever anyone turns to the Lord, the veil is taken away. Now the Lord is the Spirit, and where the Spirit of the Lord is, there is freedom."
>
> 2 Corinthians 3:14-17

Don't do that

Let me put it like this. If you tell your children not to do something, they tend to do it anyway. You don't have to teach your children to disobey you.

If you teach the ten commandments, you are bound to be drawn to disobey them.

Don't touch the stove, you tell your child, then you hear a scream. I told you not to touch it. Why did you do it anyway?

If you focus on the freedom you have in Christ and what He did for you on the cross and resurrection, then you start to do right in response to God's action.

I had a guy tell me that he struggles with an anger issue. The more he focused on the anger issue, the angrier he got. I said that's the problem. Don't focus on the anger issue, focus on knowing Christ and the anger issue will start to fade away.

I often tell guys; I'm not going to get on to you for the things you are doing wrong. I won't tell you it's alright, I just can't promise you that if you keep coming to church, keep serving, keep growing and staying connected, that you will still be doing those things a year from now.

Now if you are still doing them a year or ten years from now, we probably need to talk.

Here's a warning to those of you who want to follow the Law of Moses.

"For whoever keeps the whole law and yet stumbles at just one point is guilty of breaking all of it. For He who said, "Do not commit adultery," also said, "Do not murder." If you do not commit adultery, but do commit murder, you have become a lawbreaker."[34]

"That's too much pressure for me. Jesus said my yoke is easy and my burden is light. Apostle Paul said there is no condemnation for those who are in Christ Jesus."[35]

The other day I was driving down the street. A car was going slow obviously trying to stay below the speed limit. He was holding me up (Don't judge me) but when we got near the light it turned yellow and then red. Instead of stopping for the light the person sped up and ran the light. Now just because he kept the speed limit, he was still guilty of breaking the law because he ran the red light.

It is impossible to keep the whole law. That's why God sent Jesus to redeem us. This doesn't give us freedom to sin but to respond in love because of the gratitude we have for Him.

Why don't I teach the ten commandments? Because you are then bound to break them. I would rather teach you the freedom you have in Christ. As you are transformed into His likeness, you will start acting like Him. You'll love more, be full of more joy, more peace, more generosity. That's true transformation.

In the last chapter, we will talk about the results or the fruit of spiritual maturity. If you will focus on Knowing Jesus and being transformed, the result will be keeping His commandments.

Jesus said the entire law could be summed up with love your God and love others. Let's focus on unconditional love above everything else.

I'm not saying you will change overnight. Cut yourself some slack. Just like the boat, keep adjusting the rope. As you continue to renew your

---

34. James 2:10-11
35. Romans 8:1

mind your thinking will change. You will align your thinking with God's will for your life.

God's precepts

What is a precept? It's a general rule intended to regulate behavior or thought. Biblically, it's God's commandments and rules.

I am not against following God's commandments. What I am expressing is that if God's chosen people couldn't follow His commandments, why do we think we can do any better on our own?

The law was there to show us we needed a savior. Hebrews shares how the law was only a shadow of the good things that were to come.

If we try to follow them, we will most likely fail. But if we accept Jesus as our savior and receive the Holy Spirit, then He will transform us into His image and His law will be written on our hearts. We will do them as an outflow from our hearts.

God says,

"I will put my laws in their minds and write them on their hearts."[36]

Isaiah shares the coming good news about Jesus. Therefore, thus says the Lord GOD:

"Behold, I lay in Zion a stone for a foundation, A tried stone, a precious cornerstone, a sure foundation; Whoever believes will not act hastily."[37]

Jesus is that cornerstone!

The prophet goes on to share how God is the best teacher. He instructs us with the right judgment. He is wonderful in counsel and excellent in guidance.

---

36. Hebrews 8:10
37. Isaiah 28:16

His burden is light

Jesus recognized that the Jewish leaders had put heavy burdens on His people. Like an Oxen plowing the field, they were carrying a heavy yoke on their backs and struggling through life.

Jesus came to set us free. He said,

> "Come to me, all you who are weary and burdened, and I will give you rest. Take my yoke upon you and learn from me, for I am gentle and humble in heart, and you will find rest for your souls. For my yoke is easy and my burden is light."
>
> Matthew 11:28-30

Peter said,

"Cast all your anxiety on Him because He cares for you."[38]

You must release it to God and let it go. You must trust that God is faithful and will do what He promises.

Jesus put it this way,

"Therefore, I tell you, do not worry about your life, what you will eat or drink; or about your body, what you will wear. Is not life more than food, and the body more than clothes? Look at the birds of the air; they do not sow or reap or store away in barns, and yet your heavenly Father feeds them. Are you not much more valuable than they? Can any one of you by worrying add a single hour to your life."[39]

Next time you are tempted to worry, look around you. The birds aren't worried. You were made in God's image. You are a Child of God. He provides for the birds. How much more will He provide for you?

---

38. *1 Peter 5:7*
39. *Matthew 6:25-27*

Raise the white flag

The key is complete surrender.

James said to Humble yourselves before the Lord, and he will lift you up.[40]

The white flag is known internationally as the sign of surrender. Usually, an army would raise the white flag to surrender in battle or to request a truce to discuss conditions.

The good news is that because of what Jesus did for you and me by dying on a cross and being raised again to life, He defeated all the enemy forces of sin, death and the grave. We already have the victory. God has already won the battle.

So why surrender? Pride has already been defeated. But unless we surrender all to God, we can still be fighting battles we don't need to fight.

When we surrender all to God, we say that Jesus is Lord, and we are not. We submit ourselves to God, and He will lift us up.

Jesus said, "The thief comes only to steal and kill and destroy."[41]

Jesus goes on to say, "I have come that they may have life, and have it to the full."

Therefore God exalted him to the highest place and gave him the name that is above every name, that at the name of Jesus every knee should bow, in heaven and on earth and under the earth, and every tongue acknowledge that Jesus Christ is Lord, to the glory of God the Father.

Philippians 2:9-11

Every knee will bow before God. The question is, are you going to bow now while you have time or later when it's too late?

When we surrender all to God, we position ourselves for Him to fight our battles for us.

Here are the lyrics to I surrender all:[42]

---

40. *James 4:10*
41. *John 10:10*
42. *I Surrender All, Judson W. Van DeVenter, Published 1896 (Public domain)*

All to Jesus I surrender,
All to Him I freely give; I will ever love and trust Him, In His presence daily live.

I surrender all,
I surrender all;
All to Thee, my blessed Savior, I surrender all.
All to Jesus I surrender,
Humbly at His feet I bow; Worldly pleasures all forsaken, Take me, Jesus, take me now.

All to Jesus I surrender,
Make me, Savior, wholly Thine; Let me feel the Holy Spirit,
Truly know that Thou art mine.

All to Jesus I surrender,
Lord, I give myself to Thee;
Fill me with Thy love and power,

Let Thy blessing fall on me.
All to Jesus I surrender, Now I feel the sacred flame; Oh, the joy of full salvation!
Glory, glory, to His Name!
The real question is, are you going to bow now while you have time or later when it's too late. The choice is yours - for now.

Prayer

Lord, I surrender all to you. I need your help and ask for you to guide me. Break any pride from me and help me to become more like you. I need you to lift me up. Search my heart and reveal to me anything hidden that needs to change. Help me to become everything You created me to be. In Jesus name.

Now, cut yourself some slack and keep moving forward. Take it a day at a time. You can do it!

Chapter Seven

CHANGE YOUR MIND

> Do not conform to the pattern of this world, but be transformed by the renewing of your mind. Then you will be able to test and approve what God's will is—his good, pleasing and perfect will.
>
> Romans 12:2

My good friend Erik and I started meeting each week near the church for lunch to talk about the Bible. I always looked forward to our discussions.

I had recently heard a well-known mega-church pastor share that the church had failed in making disciples. That lit a fire in me to find out how to effectively disciple people.

One time Erik said, John, the more I study scripture, the more I am convinced that Knowing Christ is the most important thing. He shared how in Ephesians 1, Paul prayed specifically that we might know Him better.

"I keep asking that the God of our Lord Jesus Christ, the glorious Father, may give you the Spirit of wisdom and revelation, so that you may know him better.

I pray that the eyes of your heart may be enlightened in order that you may know the hope to which he has called you, the riches of his glorious inheritance in his holy people, and his incomparably great power for us who believe."[43]

What's the main thing?

Apostle Paul said, "I want to know Christ - yes, to know the power of his resurrection and participation in his sufferings, becoming like him in his death."[44]

Want to change your mind? Make KNOWING CHRIST your primary focus!

What's the secret?

Again, Paul said, "I have learned the secret of being content in any and every situation, whether well fed or hungry, whether living in plenty or in want."[45]

The Secret of being content comes through Jesus. As you know Him you are changed. Apostle Paul goes on to say,

> "I can do all this through him who gives me strength."
> Philippians 4:13

Do you want more peace in your life? It comes from the inside out. As you get to Know Jesus better, you will supernaturally experience more peace in your life. Things that rock you right now won't impact you to the same degree in the future. It's not that you won't experience struggles, but when you do you will deal with them differently.

---

43. *Ephesians 1:17-18*
44. *Philippians 3:10*
45. *Philippians 4:12*

Context matters

After my divorce, I opened my house up for Bible study. I asked Erik to come teach and invited others to come as well. I would always say, even if no one else came, I was going to sit at Jesus' feet and understand the Bible. Eventually sixty people were crammed into my house, with people even lined up along the stairs.

Erik said, the Bible never meant what it never meant. You need to ask yourself what it meant to the person who wrote it and consider who he was writing it to and what issue they were addressing. Then you can apply this to your life based on its true meaning.

As I started understanding the Bible better in context, my personal transformation accelerated. It also made me more excited and passionate about what I was hearing. My faith was increasing.

The Bible says,

"Consequently, faith comes from hearing the message, and the message is heard through the word about Christ."[46]

Before you give your life to Jesus and receive the Holy Spirit, it is challenging to read and understand scripture. But something happens when your eyes are opened to the Bible's true meaning. It changes you from the inside out.

The Apostle Paul said,

"But whenever anyone turns to the Lord, the veil is taken away. Now the Lord is the Spirit, and where the Spirit of the Lord is, there is freedom. And we all, who with unveiled faces contemplate the Lord's glory, are being transformed into his image with ever-increasing glory, which comes from the Lord, who is the Spirit."[47]

As we think about God and what he did through Jesus, we are being changed into his image. The eyes of our hearts are opened to receive God's word.

---

46. *Romans 10:17*
47. *2 Corinthians 3:16-18*

Understanding the Bible

As I was growing, I started reading N.T. Wright's[48] books and even using them as my morning devotional. What I really like about his teaching and explanation is how he explains God's story as a narrative.

> "This is not just about 'good behavior'. Rather, the lives of those who follow Jesus' act as signposts – signs that point the way to life in the Kingdom of Heaven that has now arrived on earth in Jesus the King."
>
> N.T. Wright

From creation and the garden of Eden to Jesus' return, the resurrection, and the new heaven and new earth, everything within scripture fits.

It also made me appreciate Joel Osteen and his messages even more because what people sometimes say are simple messages are in line theologically with what I was learning.

- Jesus redeemed us through his death and resurrection
- He sent the Holy Spirit to us
- We have been adopted
- We are now God's Children
- He is transforming us into His image
- One day we will reign and rule with Jesus
- Heaven's not the end of the story

Today, twenty-five plus years after being saved and becoming a member at Lakewood Church, I am getting more out of Joel Osteen's messages now than ever before. I am excited every Sunday to learn and grow. And through his message of hope, I am seeing more and more unchurched people turning to the Lord.

---

48. *N. T. Wright, New Testament Scholar, University of Oxford*

Memorizing scripture

As I mentioned, my divorce was very traumatic for me personally. It was so challenging I couldn't think right. I felt so anxious that I was sweating. I started losing weight. Lots of weight. I don't recommend the divorce diet.

One day, I sat down and memorized Philippians 4:6-7. It says,

> "Do not be anxious about anything, but in every situation, by prayer and petition, with thanksgiving, present your requests to God. And the peace of God, which transcends all understanding, will guard your hearts and your minds in Christ Jesus."

Things didn't change right away but every time I felt anxious, I would say, God Your word says, "Be anxious for nothing ..."

Pretty soon I started experiencing "the peace of God that surpasses all understanding". Now, if I even start to feel anxious, I know what to do. I speak God's word, and it changes things.

Work God's Word because God's Word works

That's the power of the Word of God. It is active. What does it mean to work the word? Use the Word of God to impact your life. Speak it out.

> "Put the word of God in you when you don't need it so, it will come out when you do."
>
> John Osteen

I'm a pretty simple guy, so before this struggle, I would usually memorize short scriptures like:
- I can do all things through Christ who strengthens me.
- The one who is in you is greater than the one who is in the world

- In all these things we are more than conquerors through him who loved us
- Be strong in the Lord and in the power of His might
- No weapon formed against you shall prosper

There's nothing wrong with collecting and memorizing your favorite verses. But when you go through something, find the scripture that specifically encourages you in your unique circumstances. Stand firm on that word. Start declaring it over your situation.

I love the story about Momma Dodie Osteen when she was diagnosed with cancer and only given a few weeks to live. She would stand on the Bible and say I am standing on the word of God. Every day she would proclaim what God said about healing. Decades later she is still sharing her testimony and encouraging others about her healing.

It's difficult to measure how someone is progressing in renewing their mind until later when we see the fruit of transformation. One milestone we can measure is memorizing scripture.

Limiting thoughts

What are you thinking about?

If you're constantly meditating on God's goodness, thinking about what He has done for you, and talking about how He has blessed you, then you're going to see God's favor in amazing ways.

The scriptures tell us this is the right direction for our minds to go in.

> Finally, brothers and sisters, whatever is true, whatever is noble, whatever is right, whatever is pure, whatever is lovely, whatever is admirable - if anything is excellent or praiseworthy - think about such things.
>
> Philippians 4:8

Take your thoughts captive

Paul says,

"We demolish arguments and every pretension that sets itself up against the knowledge of God, and we take captive every thought to make it obedient to Christ."[49]

Dr. Caroline Leaf says, "God designed humans to observe our own thoughts, catch those that are bad, and get rid of them."[50]

Here's the Freedom Formula:

1. **Identify those negative thoughts**

    Take inventory of your thought life. Write down the negative labels you think or even believe about yourself. This could be things like, you'll never amount to anything or you're a disappointment.

2. **Take negative thoughts captive**

    To do this, we must recognize those thoughts when they enter our awareness and erase them. Picture yourself grabbing those negative thoughts.

    Now, how do we replace them?

3. **To erase the negative thought**, we are going to replace them with what God says about you. Find what God says about you in His Word.

    You may have already identified some of these in the labels exercise.

---

49. *2 Corinthians 10:5*
50. *Dr. Caroline Leaf, Switch on Your Brain, 2007*

ERASE & REPLACE

Freedom milestone:
As part of renewing your mind, I encourage you to memorize at least ten scriptures from the list provided.

If you memorize one scripture a week during your one-year journey, you will have memorized 52 scriptures *(I've included the memorization scriptures in the back of this book).*

YOUR THOUGHTS INVENTORY

This week, take inventory of your thoughts. What are you thinking about? What percentage of your thoughts are negative versus positive?

Negative Thoughts   **Positive Thoughts**

Negative % _____   Positive % _____

Now that you've identified your negative thoughts, take them captive. We are going to erase our negative thoughts and replace them with what God says about us.

Write down some of the things God says about you.

Example: If your thoughts tell you, "You're not good enough", take that thought captive, erase it and replace it with I am good enough, "I am a Child of God".

Chapter Eight

FIRST THINGS FIRST

It's funny how when I look at the clock how many times I see it at 6:33. I don't see it at 6:29 or 6:40, I see it at 6:33. Morning and night it seems like God is speaking to me in the small things. It's His little reminder to me that He is present.

Matthew 6:33 says,

"Seek first the Kingdom of God and all His righteousness, and everything you need will be given unto you."

God is speaking to you in the little things. As we appreciate Him in the little things and seek Him in everything we do, He says that He is directing our steps. Sometimes we just need to sit still and listen.

Setting the tone

One way for you to seek Him first is to spend time with Him at the beginning of your day.

IT SETS THE TONE FOR YOUR DAY

When I spend time with Him first thing in the morning it changes things. I feel grounded. I am establishing myself on the Rock of Jesus.

The Wise and Foolish Builders
(Read Matthew 7:24-29)

At the sermon on the mound, Jesus shared the story about the wise and foolish builders[51]

"Therefore everyone who hears these words of mine and puts them into practice is like a wise man who built his house on the rock. The rain came down, the streams rose, and the winds blew and beat against that house; yet it did not fall, because it had its foundation on the rock.

But everyone who hears these words of mine and does not put them into practice is like a foolish man who built his house on sand.

The rain came down, the streams rose, and the winds blew and beat against that house, and it fell with a great crash".

Build your house on the Rock by putting God's Word in you and putting it into practice.

Early in the morning

Jesus set the example by consistently getting alone with God and spending time with him. Here's a few examples:[52]

- Very early in the morning, while it was still dark, Jesus got up, left the house and went off to a solitary place, where he prayed.
- When Jesus heard about John, He withdrew by boat privately to a solitary place. But the crowds found out about it and followed Him on foot from the towns.
- After He had sent them away, He went up on the mountain by Himself to pray. When evening came, He was there alone
- At daybreak, Jesus went out to a solitary place, and the crowds were looking for Him. They came to Him and tried to keep Him from leaving.
- Yet He frequently withdrew to the wilderness to pray.

One day as I was talking to a group of men about the importance of your devotional time and giving God the first part of your day. A man raised

---

51. Matthew 7:24-29
52. Mark 1:35; Matthew 14:13; Matthew 14:23; Luke 4:42; Luke 5:16

his hand and asked if he could go to the bathroom first? I said, God wants your whole heart. If you sit or kneel there needing to pee, you aren't going to be focused on Him. Go to the bathroom, make yourself a cup of coffee, and then spend some time with Him before you head out the door.

Grounding your day

My good friend Craig Johnson[53] always asks how my devotional life is going. He says,

> **"Your devotional life determines your emotional life"**

When you start your day with Jesus, it grounds us. It puts things in perspective and prepares you for anything that might come your way.

That's why,

YOUR DEVOTIONAL LIFE IS A KEY TO FREEDOM

Paul said, "So then, just as you received Christ Jesus as Lord, continue to live your lives in him, rooted and built up in him, strengthened in the faith as you were taught, and overflowing with thankfulness."[54]

When you stay grounded, your roots go deep. You won't be washed up and down with the waves of life. You will live from a place of overflow.

Sitting at the feet of Jesus

Nothing is more valuable to *Your Freedom Journey* than spending time with Jesus.

The more you "tune in" to God, the more you will hear from him.

---

53. *Craig Johnson, Lead Vertically, 2011*
54. *Colossians 2:6-7*

Pastor Craig calls it, "Tuning in to God's Frequency". When you spend time with God, you are directed by Him. You hear from Him because you have taken time to sit still and listen.

A lesson from Mary and Martha

Jesus went to the home of Mary and Martha.

Martha was busy running around the house making sure everything was in order. What she was doing was good. She was serving. I'm sure she was fixing a meal, making sure they had something to drink. She was distracted with her busyness and didn't have time to enjoy her guests.

Meanwhile, Mary sat at the feet of Jesus and listened to His words.

She was focused on Him.

Martha shared her frustration with Jesus and even asked Him to tell her to help her.

Jesus said to her,

"Martha, Martha, you are worried and troubled about many things. But one thing is needed, and Mary has chosen that good part, which will not be taken away from her."[55]

Notice how Mary was focused on Jesus and listening to his word. That's what we should do during our devotional time. Then we can spend time serving others with the right heart.

What is Devotional Time? Devotion is the object of one's affection. It's an act of prayer or private worship. Look at what you spend the most time focused on and you will see the object of your affection.

Is time with Jesus a priority for you? Our primary focus should be about spending time with God.

---

55. *Luke 10:38-42*

Prayer produces intimacy

When you pray with someone there is a spiritual connection made. That's why I will tell single men who are separated from their children to pray for them. There is no distance in prayer.

I was in a small group with my friend Tim. The mother of his child took off to another state and wouldn't let him see her. We started praying and asking God to work it out. He wanted custody and to be with her every day. I told him what I'm telling you. Pray for her every day.

It didn't happen overnight. In fact, for years I would check in with him and say, "I'm still in agreement". One day, a miracle happened. He was given custody, and she came back to Texas. He shared with me how when they got together after all these years it was like no time had passed.

It's also why we try as much as possible to have men pray with men and women with women.

In the same way, spending time in prayer with God will produce intimacy with Him. Don't make it complicated. Simply sit with Him and talk to Him like a friend. Share what's on your heart. Ask Him for wisdom. Give Him your worries. He cares about you.

Praise precedes the victory

My wife usually gets up before me and I'll hear her getting ready in the bathroom singing and praising God. She loves to put on the worship from Lakewood's Sunday service.

I will eventually join her, and we will do our devotional time together. We will praise God, spend time in prayer together and read God's word.

Worshiping God is part of our morning devotional time. We praise Him throughout the day. We don't do it because we must; we do it because we want to.

The cart before the horse

There is a saying, don't put the cart before the horse. That means you need to put the right things in the right order. It doesn't make any sense to put the cart before the horse, and that's exactly the point. Sometimes, we do things backwards.

> "For it is by grace you have been saved, through faith
> – and this is not from yourselves, it is the gift of God –
> not by works, so that no one can boast."
>
> Ephesians 2:8-9

After my mom died, my dad said to me, mom's good outweighed her bad. I told him yes; she did a lot of good. But you know what's even better dad? She knew Jesus.

That's why we say you don't have to clean yourself up first before coming to the Lord. God accepts you just the way you are.

Many religions are rules driven. If you want to go to heaven when you die, your good deeds need to outweigh your bad. The sad thing is that's not the Truth. Now we should all try to do good in life. But the point is, we can't do it on our own.

The Israelites were God's chosen people. Time after time, they failed to live up to the standard God had set for them.

Relationship with God

Through Jesus Christ, we can now have a relationship with God. Just like Adam and Eve in the original garden, God gave His only son that you might have life to the fullest.

A friend of mine told me a story about the day she was sick and tired of being sick and tired. She was ready to surrender her life to God. She pulled into a church parking lot. She was nervous and lit up one last cigarette before going inside. A woman came up to her car and tapped on the window. My friend rolled it down and the lady said, how dare you smoke at the church. Don't you know smoking is a sin? My friend responded, last time I looked gluttony was a sin. She put her car in drive and left without going inside. Years later, she did give her life to the Lord and attends a church faithfully now.

Don't be like that lady. You never know what someone is going through. You don't want to be the reason they don't come to God.

Pastor John Osteen would say, smoking won't keep you out of heaven, it will just get you there quicker.

At the end of the day, we have all sinned and fallen short of God's standard. That's why we need Jesus. It's also why I am slow to judge others. It's not my place and it's only because of the grace of God that I am not in their situation.

When you put Jesus first place in your life, you start to become like Him and start to act like Him. You will love people more, have more joy, and experience more peace.

You can't force yourself to love people more but as you become more like Christ, you will love them more. When you mess up, don't beat yourself up. Say, God, you know I messed up, I know I messed up. Please help me to know your son Jesus better.

What's your problem? Not to minimize what you are going through, but it really doesn't matter because the answer to your problem is always Jesus.

Ask for wisdom

I'd rather start my day asking God for wisdom than during the day asking God to clean up a mess I made because I didn't use wisdom.

> "If any of you lacks wisdom, you should ask God, who gives generously to all without finding fault, and it will be given to you."
>
> James 1:5

When Solomon became King after his father David died, God appeared to him in a dream and said, "Ask for whatever you want me to give you."

I am not sure how I would have responded but I am thankful for Solomon's example of how we should respond to that question.

Solomon said, "Give your servant a discerning heart to govern your people and to distinguish between right and wrong. For who is able to govern this great people of yours?"[56]

God was pleased with Solomon's request and said, "Since you have asked for this and not for long life or wealth for yourself, nor have asked for the death of your enemies but for discernment in administering justice, I will do what you have asked. I will give you a wise and discerning heart, so that there will never have been anyone like you, nor will there ever be.

Moreover, I will give you what you have not asked for—both wealth and honor - so that in your lifetime you will have no equal among kings. And if you walk in obedience to me and keep my decrees and commands as David your father did, I will give you a long life."

Wow! He put first things first and got everything else too. See as we put God first place in our lives, He goes above and beyond in our lives.

---

56. *1 King 3:9*

Leaving margin

On the seventh day, God rested.

He had spent six days creating the universe. Giving us light. Animals. And creating us.

Each day He would stop, look at what He had created and say, it was "good". At the end of the sixth day, after He made us, God said: it was very good.

"God saw all that he had made, and it was very good. And there was evening, and there was morning—the sixth day."[57]

"By the seventh day, God had finished the work he had been doing; so on the seventh day he rested from all his work."[58]

Are you leaving some room in your life for rest? It is challenging to find peace without spending time with God.

We need to recharge our batteries.

Take a deep breath

It can be challenging to slow down and enjoy the moment. I try to have a rhythm throughout the day and each week where I take breaks. I leave some margin to rest and not be exhausting myself. I get a good night's sleep.

There is a technique that helps me relax and slow down my heart rate. It helps me be in the moment.

Take a deep breath through your nose. Hold it for three seconds and then slowly exhale through your mouth. Do that a few times. Feels good right?

Take some time throughout your day to take a deep breath and enjoy the moment.

---

57. *Genesis 1:31*
58. *Genesis 2:2*

Rest! Rest! Rest!

Vow to unplug all electronics by a certain hour each night and keep your room cool to ensure a good night's rest.

Research shows that the optimal temperature for sleep is between 60- and 67-degrees Fahrenheit, with a total of 8-10 hours of sleep each night for adults.

Make sure you leave margin in your life for rest:
- Prioritizing sleep enhances cognitive function, emotional regulation, and physical health.
- Taking a weekly recovery day (Sabbath) reduces burnout and improves overall well-being.
- Periodic vacations or sabbaticals boost creativity, motivation, and long-term productivity while lowering stress.

This reminds me of Mark 6:31, where Jesus told His disciples:

"Come with me by yourselves to a quiet place and get some rest."

Rest isn't just a luxury - it's essential. How do you personally prioritize rest in your daily or weekly routine? It's not too late to start.

Making it a lifestyle

As you take time throughout the day to recognize God's presence, it becomes a natural part of our lives. And as you find a rhythm of rest, you will be more refreshed and effective.

I talk to God throughout the day and ask Him for His wisdom. I see Him and His goodness in nature and that brings me to a place of continual awareness.

He is leading, guiding and directing my steps. He wants to do the same for you!

"Trust in the LORD with all your heart and lean not on your own understanding; in all your ways submit to him, and he will make your paths straight."[59]

The important thing is to recognize Him throughout the day.

---

59. *Proverbs 3:5-6*

Chapter Nine

WHAT ARE YOU SAYING?

And God said, "Let there be light, and there was light."[60] God spoke the world into existence.

Then God said, "Let us make mankind in our image, in our likeness, so that they may rule over the fish in the sea and the birds in the sky, over the livestock and all the wild animals, and over all the creatures that move along the ground."[61] You were created in God's image.

Your words have creative power. What kind of world are you creating?

> "The tongue has the power of life and death, and those who love it will eat its fruit."
>
> Proverbs 18:21

If what you were saying happened, would you be glad or sad?

We took inventory of our thoughts. Now pay attention to your words. What are you saying? What do I mean? I hear people say things like, you're killing me or I'm dead. They don't really mean that, but it's become part of our daily language.

I'll also hear people say, I have cancer and probably won't make it. I don't want to make light of how scary that is but is that really what you want? Of course not.

If death and life are really in the power of the tongue, then we need to watch our words. Are you speaking life to your situation?

---

60. *Genesis 1:3*
61. *Genesis 1:26*

The Tongue is Powerful

James said, "When we put bits into the mouths of horses to make them obey us, we can turn the whole animal. Or take ships as an example. Although they are so large and are driven by strong winds, they are steered by a very small rudder wherever the pilot wants to go. Likewise, the tongue is a small part of the body, but it makes great boasts. Consider what a great forest is set on fire by a small spark".[62]

He gave us three examples:

1. Bits in the mouth of horses

If you've ever gone horseback riding, you know how important the bit is. The bit goes into the horse's mouth and attaches to the headstall so that you can control its movements. Without it the horse would go where it wants but with a small pull back on the reins the horse stops.

2. A ship's rudder

Laura and I were sailing on a catamaran in the Caribbean Ocean. With a strong wind, you can get moving fast. With one small turn of the rudder, I could turn the sailboat with little effort. One time I turned it so fast that Laura fell back into the water. Steering the rudder to go back to get her was a little more challenging but within minutes she was safe and sound.

3. Spark ignites a forest fire

I love campfires. When I was young, I would go on camping trips. I would always help build the fire and put some tinder under the logs to help them catch fire. It can be challenging to get the fire started especially if you don't have matches. But after you create a spark and the tinder catches on fire, it's amazing how fast it spreads. If you aren't careful, you can catch an entire forest on fire.

---

62. *James 3:3-5*

In the same way, our tongue is small but strong. Like a bit in the horse's mouth, it can choose to speak or hold back and stay silent, like a ship's rudder, it can determine the course of our lives. It can choose to say positive or negative things. And like a small spark, it can harm people and engage in heated arguments.

A miracle in your mouth

One of the reasons I watch my words is because it impacts my faith. If I go around saying things I don't really mean, then when I do mean it, my mind doesn't know what to believe.

For instance, if I go around saying you're killing me when you tell a joke or when you mess up, then when I want to speak life to someone in the hospital, I might not have the faith for it to happen.

But if I watch my words and am careful to only speak life, then I believe my prayers will be powerful and effective.

There's a miracle in your mouth. There is someone who needs to hear something positive. People need encouragement. To be built up. We all hear enough discouraging words from people. You can't do that. You'll never amount to anything. Why don't you be different? Speak life into someone. Who can you encourage today?

It doesn't have to be in person. You can send a text, write on a sticky note, or call someone you haven't talked to in a while. We all need what you have to offer.

Miracle Maker

Did you know as a believer, you are a miracle maker? God wants to bring healing to others but He's working through us to do it.

Do you believe that God is still doing miracles today? Do you believe He can use you to perform them? My challenge to you today is to be bold enough to pray for someone who needs a miracle.

You might say, what if He doesn't heal them? What if He does? That's what faith is, stepping out of our comfort zone of the possible so God can do the impossible.

Hold your tongue

The wisest man who ever lived was Solomon. In the book of Proverbs[63] he said,

- When words are many, sin is unavoidable, but he who restrains his lips is wise.
- An evil man is trapped by his rebellious speech, but a righteous man escapes from trouble.
- From the fruit of his lips a man enjoys good things, but the desire of the faithless is violence.
- He who guards his mouth protects his life, but the one who opens his lips invites his own ruin.
- He who guards his mouth and tongue keeps his soul from distress.
- The words of the reckless pierce like swords, but the tongue of the wise brings healing.

It's wise to hold your tongue. There are so many things in life that are out of our control. We can't control what other people say but we can control what we say. When we can restrain ourselves and not respond.

If you can't say something nice, don't say anything at all. If I've heard that saying once, I've heard it a thousand times. I'm sure you have too. But what if we took that to heart and only said positive things? It takes self-control to not complain, blame, say negative or hurtful things. It is possible.

---

63. *Proverbs 10:19; 12:13; 13:2; 13:3; 21:23; 12:18*

Your words are seeds

When you speak, your words go into someone else's ears. They plant seeds. When you tell someone, they can become something great, it plants seeds in their hearts and minds. When you believe in someone and continue to encourage them, you are watering those seeds. Too many people tear people down.

There can be negative seeds too. Maybe a parent told you something negative when you were growing up. Did you let it take root? It takes time for something to take root. Maybe you heard it repeatedly. Over time you started to internalize it. You started believing something negative about yourself.

Speak God's promises

Remind God of His promises. Whatever you are going through, find where it is written in the Bible and then turn God's word into your prayer.

> For no matter how many promises God has made, they are "Yes" in Christ. And so through him the "Amen" is spoken by us to the glory of God.
>
> 2 Corinthians 1:20

God said, "Put Me in remembrance; Let us contend together; State your *case,* that you may be acquitted."[64]

God watches over His Word to perform it.

Then the LORD said to me, "You have seen well, for I am ready to perform My word."[65]

Joel Osteen shared that "God is not obligated to bring to pass what you say but He is obligated to bring to pass what He says. When he hears

---

64. Isaiah 43:26
65. Jeremiah 1:12

His promise come out of your mouth angels go to work. Favor is released. Miracles are set into motion."

> "Even though all the promises of God belong to you, you won't experience them if you can't receive them. Any truth you can't receive is a truth that won't set you free."[66]
>
> Phillip Hunter

Find where it is written and speak it out

What are you going through? Are you experiencing a health, financial, family or other issue? Find where God made a promise in the area of your problem and remind Him of His promise. His promises are Yes and Amen.

God, you promised _____

Stand on His Promise.

People builders

Paul said, "Do not let any unwholesome talk come out of your mouths, but only what is helpful for building others up according to their needs, that it may benefit those who listen."[67]

And again, he tells believers,

> "Therefore encourage one another and build each other up, just as in fact you are doing."[68]

---

66. Philip Hunter, *The Promise Principle: A New Way to Encounter the Bible*, 2017
67. *Ephesians 4:29*
68. *1 Thessalonians 5:11*

Do your words benefit others? Are you building people up? Are you building yourself up?

Use your words to create your world.

Freedom challenge

- Would I want my words to become reality? This is a convicting question because it forces us to be intentional with how we speak about ourselves, others, and our situations.
- Speaking life over others can shift atmospheres, strengthen relationships, and build faith.

YOUR WORDS INVENTORY

This week, take inventory of your words. What are you saying? What percentage of your words are negative versus positive?

Negative Words   **Positive Words**

Negative % _____   Positive % _____

You can write them down as they happen or reflect on your conversations at the end of the day.

Are you using your words to build people up or tear them down?

Would you want what you are saying to actually happen?

In some of the negative conversations, could you have held your tongue and not said anything? How would that have changed things? What could you have said or not said differently? What might you have said instead?

*** *As you become more aware of your words, practice controlling your tongue and not saying anything or saying positive constructive words. Continue the process until you don't have to watch your words anymore.* ***

Chapter Ten

THE GAME CHANGER

What's going to be different this time?

That's what people who have tried and tried and tried to overcome their struggles will often ask.

Maybe you've tried different therapies, programs, or centers. Maybe it worked for a while, but you couldn't sustain it.

The good news is, God wants to help you change. Jesus told his disciples that it was beneficial that he leaves. Because of his sacrifice, it made a way for God to pour out the Holy Spirit for all believers to receive.

Jesus said, I won't leave you as orphans. He would send the Holy Spirit. The Holy Spirit is such a powerful and essential presence in our lives.

- As our Helper, He strengthens and supports us (John 14:16).
- As our Counselor, He gives wisdom and direction (Isaiah 11:2).
- As our Teacher, He reveals truth and deepens our understanding (John 14:26).
- As our Guide, He leads us in the way we should go (Romans 8:14).
- As our Advocate, He intercedes for us and defends us (John 15:26).
- As our Seal, He marks us as God's own and secures our salvation (Ephesians 1:13-14).
- As our Edifier, He builds us up in faith (1 Corinthians 14:4).
- As our Empowerer, He gives us strength and boldness (Acts 1:8).
- As our Unifier, He brings believers together in love and purpose (Ephesians 4:3).

- As our Gift Giver, He distributes spiritual gifts for the good of the body of Christ (1 Corinthians 12:4-11).

And so much more!

The Holy Spirit isn't just a force or feeling - He is God, living in us, actively working in our lives every day.

Have you experienced a moment where you clearly felt the Holy Spirit guiding or strengthening you?

Have you heard of the Holy Spirit?

In Act 19, Apostle Paul came across a group of twelve believers. He asked them, "Did you receive the Holy Spirit when you believed?" They responded that they hadn't even heard about this Holy Spirit.

That was the case with me. I always believed in God, but I somehow made it thirty-five years without being saved.

Then one day, my brother-in-law was so excited to share about the experience he had.

I had always believed that God existed but wasn't saved. Somehow, I had escaped it for all these years. So, I desired to find out more and receive what he was so excited about.

The very next Sunday, we went to his church. It was a small Pentecostal church in Spring, Texas.

A cute older couple came up to me and said something like, you want to come up front, don't you? I did. As the leaders of the church led us in the prayer of salvation, they laid hands on me and my tongue started moving. I immediately started speaking in what is known as our personal prayer language.

I didn't know any better and hadn't been taught any denominational warnings against the Baptism of the Holy Spirit, so I just received this gift with joy. I had received my Helper.

I can tell you this, I wouldn't want to go through this Christian life without the Baptism of the Holy Spirit with evidence of speaking in tongues. I need a Helper! How about you?

The good news is when we give our lives to Jesus, we don't have to go through life alone. Jesus said he wouldn't leave us as orphans. But he would send the Holy Spirit to lead us, to guide us and to direct our steps.

While there is a lot of confusion about this gift, I have tried to explain it as simply as I can here for you. My hope is that you will pray and ask God for this gift.

The perfect prayer

When you don't know what to pray, you can pray in the spirit. The Bible says, when we speak in tongues, we pray spirit to spirit with God. You are praying a perfect prayer.

"In the same way, the Spirit helps us in our weakness. We do not know what we ought to pray for, but the Spirit himself intercedes for us through wordless groans."[69]

It also says, you are edifying or improving yourself. "Anyone who speaks in a tongue edifies themselves."[70]

That's your Helper going to work on your behalf.

The Spirit of Elijah

Let's start with an Old Testament example. Unlike today, before Jesus, the Holy Spirit would come on certain individuals like the prophets and kings for the fulfillment of God's purposes. Elijah was one of those prophets.

You think we've got it bad today? Elijah lived in the days of King Ahab and Jezebel. Jezebel went around killing all of God's prophets. You would think that would cause Elijah to shrink back in fear. And he did have his moments. Just like we all do.

---

69. *Romans 8:26*
70. *1 Corinthians 14:4*

But Elijah proclaimed God's word boldly before the king. God's people are lukewarm and worshiping Baals. Worthless gods. Not the one true God.

God had told them in Deuteronomy 28 that as long as you obey my commands, I will bless you. But if you turn to other idols, I will curse you. I will close off the heavens and you will receive no rain. And that's exactly what happened at Elijah's word and it didn't rain for 3 1/2 years.

Well, you might think that's great for Elijah. He was Elijah after all. We might be tempted to put him on a pedestal.

But James 5:17 says,

"Elijah was a human being, even as we are. He prayed earnestly that it would not rain, and it did not rain on the land for three and a half years".

Miracle working power

Here are some of the miracles from Elijah:

- Caused the rain the cease for 3 1/2 years
- Fed by the ravens
- Miracle of the jar of flour and jug of oil not running out during famine
- Resurrection of the widow's son
- Calling of fire from heaven on the altar
- Caused it to rain again
- His Prophecy that Jezebel would be eaten by dogs. What a way to go!
- Parting of the Jordan River
- His Prophecy that Elisha should have a double portion of his spirit
- Being caught up to heaven in a whirlwind. What a better way to GO!

Do you know how Elijah did so many miracles? He believed God would do what He said he would do. It's not by our power, but the power of the living God. That's what faith is all about.

The game changer

Now, because of what Jesus did on the cross. And because he was resurrected from the dead. He became the perfect sacrifice to God. We no longer must hear God through other people, we now have direct access to God through the Holy Spirit.

Pentecost means fifty. Jesus was with them for forty days. That's why Jesus told His followers to tarry in Jerusalem. They had to wait another ten days after Jesus ascended to heaven to receive their helper.

Old Testament shadows

The time between the first Passover in Egypt when God delivered the Israelites out of slavery to the time God gave the law through Moses on Mount Sinai was fifty days.

When the law was given from Sinai, God appeared in a thick cloud. There was the sound of a ram's horn, with thunder and lightning flashes. And in smoke, like the smoke of a furnace. And the mountain was burning with fire unto the heart of the heavens. Then the Lord spoke to the Israelites in the midst of the fire."[71]

New Testament

On the day of Pentecost in Jerusalem, there was a rushing of violent wind, "Divided tongues as of fire rested on each one of them and the proclamation of the gospel was shared in unlearned languages."[72] The big difference was the Old Testament Pentecost brought the law. The New Testament Pentecost through Jesus brought grace. We have been set free from the curse of the law. We are now led by the spirit and not by the flesh.

says,

"And with that he breathed on them and said, "Receive the Holy

---

71. *Exodus 20:18*
72. *Acts 2:2*

Spirit[73]". See when you believe in Jesus you receive the Holy Spirit. But in both the old and New Testament, you receive power when the Holy Spirit comes on you" (Say "ON YOU").

In Acts 1:8, Jesus said, but you will receive power when the Holy Spirit comes on you; and you will be my witnesses in Jerusalem, and in all Judea and Samaria, and to the ends of the earth.

Then we all know what happened on the day of Pentecost. Think about Peter before the Baptism of the Holy Spirit where he denied Jesus three times to afterwards when he preached boldly to thousands and was willing to die for his faith. Sharing the words of the prophet Joël, he said, "I will pour out of My Spirit on all flesh"[74] (Say "ON").

The Acts of the Apostles

Here are some examples from Acts:

Philip in Samaria (Acts 8)

The Bible says they believed and were water baptized. Peter and John came to them. When they arrived, they prayed for them that they might receive the Holy Spirit because the Holy Spirit had not yet come upon any of them. They had simply been baptized in the name of the Lord Jesus. Then Peter and John placed their hands on them, and they received the Holy Spirit.

Cornelius the first gentile believer (Acts 10)

Now, we hear about a gentile Roman leader named Cornelius. Through a series of circumstances Peter ends up sharing the gospel to Cornelius' entire family.

The Bible says, while Peter was still speaking these words, the Holy Spirit fell upon all those who heard the word (Say ALL). And those of the circumcision who believed were astonished, as many as came with Peter,

---

73. *John 20:22*
74. *Joel 2:28*

because the gift of the Holy Spirit had been poured out on the Gentiles also. For they heard them speak with tongues and magnify God. He was the first non-Jew who spoke in tongues showing that it is for me and you.

Paul in Ephesus (Acts 19)

Apostle Paul was going through Ephesus when he came across twelve disciples or believers. As I mentioned, they had not even heard of the Holy Spirit.

When Paul had laid hands on them, the Holy Spirit came upon them, and they spoke with tongues and prophesied. Now the men were about twelve in all (Say "ALL").

Receiving the Baptism of the Holy Spirit

Jesus said, "If you then, though you are evil, know how to give good gifts to your children, how much more will your Father in heaven give the Holy Spirit to those who ask him."[75]

In case you think you can receive the Holy Spirit only one way. Over ten years ago, someone reached out to me because her boyfriend kept lying to her. He got caught cheating and gave his life to Jesus. She wanted him to receive the Baptism of the Holy Spirit.

He couldn't find anyone to help him. I said, I'll pray for him. Now he was in Dallas, and I was in Houston. But over the phone, I prayed the same simple prayer with him that we are going to pray together. And over the phone, he started speaking in tongues.

Friends don't put God in a box. Don't set limits on God.

Well, you might say, John, I've heard the Holy Spirit isn't for everyone. Well, maybe it's for you. Why don't we just ask. What's the worst thing that can happen?

---

75. Luke 11:13

You must do the talking

Now the Holy Spirit is a gentleman. We have to do the speaking. So, like turning on or off a lightbulb. At some point you're going to have to stop speaking English and speak out what your tongue is wanting to utter.

If you already have your prayer language, awesome! Do this from the perspective of sharing it with someone else. I believe God will bring someone across your path over the next week who you can pray this with. There's no better gift after salvation! Share it with someone else.

The greater gifts

Apostle Paul says to pray for the greater gifts. "Now eagerly desire the greater gifts."[76] and again, "Earnestly pursue love and eagerly desire spiritual gifts, especially the gift of prophecy."[77] God has given us gifts for the upbuilding of the church. He encourages us to pursue them.

We are going to do just that. One gift is not better than another and they are not based on something we earned. We shouldn't get puffed up and brag about our gifts.

Body of Christ

Apostle Paul says the church is a body. One part of the body isn't any more important than another. We can't eat without the mouth and tongue, but at the same time we need our arms and legs. We all have gifts, talents and abilities that benefit the body. We are truly better together.

When you ask you receive

When you ask by faith, I believe you receive it. But like with Cornelius, the evidence of receiving is the speaking in tongues.

Most people receive their prayer language right away, but there have

---

76. *1 Corinthians 12:31*
77. *1 Corinthians 14:1*

been times when people have come to me later and said, while I was on my way home worshiping God or while I was in the shower.

It just came bursting out.

When I first received, it sounded like "babababa". One day a preacher said not to me but in a message, none of this "babababa" stuff. Well, I went straight home and went into my prayer closet. I decided I wasn't leaving until out of my belly came rivers of living water. Well about three hours later my prayer language changed.

Shimaka . . .

Your thoughts

The enemy will try to tell you that it's not from God or you're not really speaking in tongues but that's common, just keep doing it. Apostle Paul taught when you speak in tongues you edify yourself. He confidently announced that he spoke in tongues more than anyone.

Are you ready to receive?

Pray this out loud:

Lord Jesus, I thank you that I am saved. . . And I Confess Jesus Christ is my Lord and Savior. . . Jesus, you promised me another helper, the Holy Spirit if I would just ask . . .

So right now, I ask for the Baptism of the Holy Spirit with evidence of speaking in tongues, in Jesus' name. Now start to praise Him.

Gifts of the Spirit

Apostle Paul said to pray for gifts to be distributed that are needed for the upbuilding of the church in Jesus' name.

Lord, you say to ask for the greater gifts. You said pray for prophecy. So right now, I ask you for the gifts you have for me. I ask for the gift of prophecy. I thank you for them and ask you to lead, guide and direct my steps. That I will be led by Your spirit and not by the flesh, in Jesus' name.

Spiritual Gifts:

- The Gift of Wisdom
- The Gift of Knowledge
- The Gift of Discernment
- The Gift of Exhortation/ Encouragement
- The Gift of Discerning
- The Gift of Faith
- The Gift of Healing
- The Gift of Miracles
- The Gift of Discerning Spirits
- The Gift of Tongues
- The Gift of Interpreting Tongues
- The Gift of Administration
- The Gift of Leadership
- The Gift of Apostleship
- The Gift of Evangelist
- The Gift of Pastor/ Shepherd
- The Gift of Teaching
- The Gift of Mercy
- The Gift of Service
- The Gift of Helps
- The Gift of Prophecy

Chapter Eleven

FROM PREY TO PRAY

When eagles hunt, they have the advantage of speed over their prey. With their incredible eyesight, they can see their prey from far above and quickly grab a fresh meal. I've watched as they've swooped down and grabbed a fish before it even knew what was going on.

On the contrary, a vulture eats any dead carcass it finds. It feeds on the sad circumstances of other animals.

We also have an enemy who likes to find opportunities to take advantage of our circumstances to get us distracted, bring division and keep us from our destiny. He wants to feed on our misery. When Jesus sent His disciples out into the world He said,

"I am sending you out like sheep among wolves. Therefore, be as shrewd as snakes and as innocent as doves."[78]

We need to be aware of the enemy's schemes if we are going to combat them.

Like the eagle, we need to use what God has given us to move from being the enemy's prey to soaring above our circumstances and being victorious. We were created to soar.

Peter said, "Be alert and of sober mind. Your enemy the devil prowls around like a roaring lion looking for someone to devour."[79]

---

78. *Matthew 10:16*
79. *1 Peter 5:8*

Our battle is not against flesh and blood

It's challenging sometimes to not get hurt or offended when people attack us and say negative things about us. It goes back to having the right perspective.

People are not your problem. The battles we have in life are not fundamentally physical. Our problem is we are fighting spiritual battles by physical means. The Bible says,

"For our struggle is not against flesh and blood, but against the rulers, against the authorities, against the powers of this dark world and against the spiritual forces of evil in the heavenly realms."[80]

Apostle Paul tells us to dress for success. He says to put on the full Armor of God so we can stand when the trials and struggles of life come against us.

I believe we are fighting many battles we don't need to fight. Battles we weren't meant to fight. Your battle is not against your wife, kids, employers or other people.

That's why we must use wisdom. God's wisdom!

He has you surrounded!

Although it seems like you are surrounded by problems and difficult circumstances, God surrounds everything that's surrounding you. You are an overcomer!

There is a powerful story in the Bible where an enemy army surrounded Elisha and his servant. Like most of us, the servant was afraid. Elisha said, don't be afraid. "Those who are for us are more than those who are against us."[81]

How many times do we react like the servant? It's only natural to see a big obstacle in front of us and be afraid. It could be a doctor's report, a bank statement, a child that's off course.

---

80. Ephesians 6:12
81. Kings 6:16

But Elisha prayed for God to open the servant's eyes to see the supernatural. Suddenly, he could see the Heavenly armies all around their enemy.

Like the servant, if we could see in the spiritual realm, we wouldn't be afraid. But faith is believing even when we can't see. We must trust that God is greater than what's going on around us.

Here are some encouraging scriptures where God is bigger than the enemy you are facing.

- "The angel of the LORD encamps around those who fear him, and he delivers them."[82]
- "Therefore, since we are surrounded by such a great cloud of witnesses, let us throw off everything that hinders and the sin that so easily entangles. And let us run with perseverance the race marked out for us, fixing our eyes on Jesus, the pioneer and perfecter of faith. For the joy set before him he endured the cross, scorning its shame, and sat down at the right hand of the throne of God."[83]
- "You are my hiding place; you will protect me from trouble and surround me with songs of deliverance."[84]
- "As the mountains surround Jerusalem, so the LORD surrounds his people both now and forevermore."[85]

Rise above your circumstances

When there is a storm, things can be chaotic. We might feel a bit out of control of our lives. With the waves crashing all around us, it's easy to get anxious, to be fearful and lose hope.

The eagle though rises higher. He goes above the clouds. Even though

---

82. *Psalm 34:7*
83. *Hebrews 12:1-2*
84. *Psalm 32:7*
85. *Psalm 125:2*

the storm is raging below, he is soaring above it all, enjoying the clear sky above.

We serve a big God. The bigger we make our God the smaller our circumstances will seem. Be like the eagle and rise above what's going on around you. God promises to fight that battle for you. That is why Paul says to dress for success. We must be intentional about how we position ourselves.

Every day before we leave the house, we need to put on God's armor.

Put on the Full Armor of God[86]

"Finally, be strong in the Lord and in his mighty power.

Put on the full armor of God, so that you can take your stand against the devil's schemes.

For our struggle is not against flesh and blood, but against the rulers, against the authorities, against the powers of this dark world and against the spiritual forces of evil in the heavenly realms.

Therefore, put on the full armor of God, so that when the day of evil comes, you may be able to stand your ground, and after you have done everything, to stand.

Stand firm then, with the belt of truth buckled around your waist, with the breastplate of righteousness in place, and with your feet fitted with the readiness that comes from the gospel of peace.

In addition to all this, take up the shield of faith, with which you can extinguish all the flaming arrows of the evil one.

Take the helmet of salvation and the sword of the Spirit, which is the word of God.

And pray in the Spirit on all occasions with all kinds of prayers and requests. Be alert and always keep on praying for all the Lord's people."

When we put on God's armor, we are positioning ourselves for the

---

86. *Ephesians 6:10-19*

day. Instead of being unarmed and open to the attack of the enemy, we are covered by God. We have intentionally prepared ourselves for victory.

Jesus came to give you life

The thief comes only to steal and kill and destroy; I have come that they may have life and have it to the full.[87]

The good news is Jesus has given us His authority.

He says,

"These signs will accompany those who believe: In my name they will drive out demons; they will speak in new tongues; they will pick up snakes with their hands; and when they drink deadly poison, it will not hurt them at all; they will place their hands on sick people, and they will get well."[88]

Spiritual weapons

The eagle is a highly effective hunter.

He has a large powerful beak designed for tearing apart prey. They use their beaks for building nests and defending themselves and their young.

The eagle has these incredibly powerful talons or claws they use to grip and tear apart their prey.

They have sharp eyesight to be able to spot their prey as far as two miles away.

And their strong and large wingspan along with their feather composition and multi-functional tails that help them fly extremely fast, turn quickly and soar for long distances.

Like the eagle, we want to use the weapons God gave us to effectively fight our spiritual battles.

"For though we live in the world, we do not wage war as the world does. The weapons we fight with are not the weapons of the world.

On the contrary, they have divine power to demolish strongholds. We

---

87. John 10:10
88. Mark 16:17-18

demolish arguments and every pretension that sets itself up against the knowledge of God, and we take captive every thought to make it obedient to Christ."[89]

"And having disarmed the powers and authorities, he made a public spectacle of them, triumphing over them by the cross."[90]

We already have the victory through Jesus. Because of His sacrifice, we now have power and authority over the enemy.

The challenge sometimes is keeping the right perspective over who the enemy is and using our authority effectively.

1. Word of God

"For the word of God is alive and active. Sharper than any double-edged sword, it penetrates even to dividing soul and spirit, joints and marrow; it judges the thoughts and attitudes of the heart."[91]

The Word of God says to bind on earth what is bound in heaven and loose on earth what is loosed in Heaven.[92]

Using God's Word, you have authority to say, devil I bind you in the name of Jesus and loose Your angels to fight this battle for me.

In Biblical terms, the word "loose" is used to mean "release" or "set into motion," especially when praying for angelic help, freedom, or God's power to be released.

2. Blood of Jesus

Because of what Jesus did by shedding his blood and rising from the dead, we don't fight for victory but from a position of victory.

In Egypt, the Israelites were told to put the blood of a lamb on the doorpost of their house and the death angel would pass over them. When

---

89. 2 Corinthians 10:3-5
90. Colossians 2:15
91. Hebrews 4:12
92. Matthew 18:18

the angel saw the blood, it wouldn't enter the home. But if the house didn't have the blood it went in and killed the first born. It wasn't about who was in the house. It was about the blood.

Jesus was our sacrificial lamb. He gave his blood as a sacrifice to take away our sins and enable us to enter God's presence.

Paul said, "and all are justified freely by his grace through the redemption that came by Christ Jesus. God presented Christ as a sacrifice of atonement, through the shedding of his blood—to be received by faith."[93]

John said in the Book of Revelations, "They triumphed over him by the blood of the Lamb and by the word of their testimony; they did not love their lives so much as to shrink from death."[94]

I will regularly plead the blood of Jesus over my house and declare God's word that any evil must pass over it. I use anointing oil which represents the presence of God.

3. The Name of Jesus

> "At the name of Jesus every knee should bow, in heaven and on earth and under the earth, and every tongue acknowledge that Jesus Christ is Lord, to the glory of God the Father."
>
> Philippians 2:10-11

Jesus Himself said "if you ask anything in my name I will do it."[95]
That means,
- cancer
- addiction
- depression

---

93. *Romans 3:24-25*
94. *Revelation 12:11*
95. *John 14:14*

- anxiety
- sickness
- devil and demon forces
- generational curses

must bow in the name of Jesus. His name is above any other name.

You don't have to pray God, if it's your will. As long as you pray His Word you are praying His will. Say, in the name of Jesus I command sickness to flee this body.

Breaking strongholds

What is a stronghold? Usually, it has to do with our thinking. We have thoughts that have rooted in our minds.

Before the invention of cars, horse drawn carriages would create paths as they traveled the same path repeatedly. Over time, a road would develop ruts so that it was hard to go any other direction than that previously traveled. That's what happens in our minds as we continue to think the same things over and over again. We can get in a rut so to speak.

The enemy wants you to think wrongly about yourself. He doesn't want you to reach your full potential. He is going to whisper things to you, have other people push your buttons or continue to have you play those wrong recordings about yourself repeatedly.

It's also been proven that we can pass these strongholds through our DNA. You may be genetically predisposed for alcohol, poverty, or depression. That's what we call generational curses.

Let it stop with you!

To be free, you need to be honest, admit your problem and confess your sin.

So how do you overcome these strongholds?

We visited this scripture earlier and it's worth repeating here:

"The weapons we fight with are not the weapons of the world. On the contrary, they have divine power to demolish strongholds. We demolish arguments and every pretension that sets itself up against the knowledge of God, and we take captive every thought to make it obedient to Christ."[96]

Strongholds often start as thought patterns or false beliefs – lies that have taken root in the mind.

According to God's Word, you need to:

- **Recognize**

  The enemy's tactics are to deceive and lie about your identity.

  To overcome our struggles, we must first recognize that we have a problem. What's the issue?

- **Repentance**

  You can do this by being honest with God and humbly allowing the Holy Spirit to expose any strongholds, sins or negative behaviors in your life.

  These also include sins of omission and commission and sins of our fathers that have been generationally passed down. Ask God for His forgiveness and release it to God.

  It's one of the reasons James said, "Therefore confess your sins to each other and pray for each other so that you may be healed."[97]

  John said, "if we confess our sins, he is faithful and just and will forgive us our sins and purify us from all unrighteousness."[98]

  Have you heard that confession is good for the soul? The reason for that is you aren't holding something toxic within you. You are letting it out. You're releasing it.

  Water that doesn't flow can become stagnant and toxic. When you

---

96. *2 Corinthians 10:4–5*
97. *James 5:16*
98. *1 John 1:9*

hold unforgiveness, shame, and shortcomings in, your body retains it. It can be toxic to your body.

The key is getting it out and letting it go.

Repentance simply means a change of direction. You must share your challenges with God and let Him change you by

His Spirit.

- **Renounce**

    We need to cast down the enemy's arguments. The key is to

    resist wrong information and fill your mind with the right information.

    James 4:7 says, "Submit yourselves, then, to God. Resist the devil, and he will flee from you."

    To renounce means to surrender the issue to God and let Him fight your battle for you. Raise the white flag of surrender.

    If you've been involved in any witchcraft or the occult, you need to also get rid of any demonic object within your possession.

- **Release yourself**

    Release yourself from any stronghold. Ask God to release you from any demonic influence, entities or soul ties.

    "Cast your cares on God because He cares for you."[99]

    Jesus said whatever you bind on earth will be bound in heaven and whatever you loose on earth will be loosed in heaven.

    You've been given the authority to cast out demons. Now take authority and command the enemy to flee.

    Say, Satan I bind you. I command you to take your hand off my family and leave now in Jesus' name. I loose the angels of heaven

---

99. *1 Peter 5:7*

to go forth and fight this battle for me. I proclaim that I already have victory in Jesus' name.

- **Replace**

  We now need to bring every thought into captivity.

  You can do this by making your thoughts obedient to Christ. You must take those wrong thoughts captive and exchange them for God's Truth. This goes back to erase and replace. Fill the empty place with God's Word.

  Remember to resist the devil, and he will flee from you.

- **Renew your mind**

  As your mind is transformed, Paul says we will be able to discern what is right.

  As our mind is changed, we will grow spiritually stronger and be able to discern and resist the enemies' schemes.

- **Remain rooted**

  Finally, start spending time with God daily through your devotional time. Keep your eyes focused on Jesus. As you do this, your mind will be renewed, and you will be rooted in Him.

  Surround yourself with Godly believers and remain planted in the House of the Lord. Stay actively involved in church.

Though the journey may feel long and challenging at times, remember that God is with you every step of the way. His patience and love for you never wavers, and He is always faithful to finish the work He has started in you.

Generational curses

Generational curses refer to patterns of negative behavior, sin, or consequences that seem to repeat themselves through family lines.

These could be anything from addiction, anger, or unforgiveness to financial struggles or broken relationships. These patterns can be passed down due to unrepented sin or unforgiveness, but through Jesus, we have the power to break free.

In the Old Testament, God shared that He would hold the sins of the father against other generations.

God said in Deuteronomy,[100]

"If you fully obey the LORD your God and carefully follow all his commands I give you today, the LORD your God will set you high above all the nations on earth. All these blessings will come on you and accompany you if you obey the LORD your God.

However, if you do not obey the LORD your God and do not carefully follow all his commands and decrees, I am giving you today, all these curses will come on you and overtake you . . ."

Because Jesus came to set us free, we don't have to settle for generational curses, you can be the one to set your family free.

It is true that these wrongs seem to cling to us unless we forgive and let them go. We need to release them to God. There are consequences for our choices that we may have to deal with. For instance, if you kill someone, you may still have to serve your time.

We all know someone whose father was abusive and then the son became just like them. He was abusive, angry, and maybe drank too much. They were hurt by it. But then they became just like him.

While the Old Testament teaches us about the consequences of disobedience, the New Testament reveals God's ultimate plan for

---

100. *Deuteronomy 28*

redemption through Jesus. In Him, the curse is broken, and freedom is offered to anyone who believes.

Dr. Caroline Leaf said,

"The sins of parents create a predisposition, not a destiny."[101]

If you feel like you are struggling with an addiction or some other life event that has been in your family for generations, I invite you to pray this with me:

Prayer:

Father God, I want to be free. Jesus, I know you came to set me free. I ask You for forgiveness for what I have done. I forgive my father (or the person who hurt me). I release them to you.

I ask you to heal me now. I break this curse from my family in the name of Jesus. And thank you for the freedom I have through your son Jesus. Thank you that me and my entire family are free in Jesus' name.

Deliverance

I don't know about you, but the word "deliverance" makes me think of scary movies where people were possessed, and it seemed like even the priests were victims to their false power. Such fiction!

It means to be "rescued". Hopefully, by now you've recognized that Jesus came to rescue you. He is our rescue hero!

He delivered you from evil. That means you already have the victory through Jesus. Now you have the authority to cast out demons in Jesus' name.

What do you need to be rescued from?

Moses rescued the Israelites from Egypt after 400 years of slavery. He delivered them from slavery, and they were baptized through their experience in the red sea. In that moment they moved from the old to the new.

---

101. Dr. Caroline Leaf, Switch on Your Brain, 2007

God wanted them to go into the promised land. It was a short journey but when they got there, they were afraid. They saw themselves like grasshoppers.

How do you see yourself?

It's hard to enter your promised land if you are holding onto the chains of your past.

They complained and wanted to go back to Egypt even if it meant being slaves again. How many times do we put up with injustice because we don't want to change? They still had a slave mentality.

You are a new creation!

You have been set free. You are a Child of God. He wants you to have a son mentality! Don't remain a slave!

They didn't get to enter their promised land and died in the desert. Don't let your dreams die with you. God wants you to be fully free to live your best life right now.

Jesus crossed the lake and came across a man living in the tombs. He was too strong for the chains people tried to put on him, but he was still in his own personal bondage.

Jesus simply said, "For Jesus had said to him, "Come out of this man, you impure spirit!"[102] Jesus has given us that same authority in His name.

I have seen first-hand that our activities in drugs and alcohol as well as participating in the occult can open the door to the enemy.

The good news is that if you have accepted Jesus as your Lord and Savior, He has given you full authority over the enemy.

I also encourage you not to entertain or open the door to demonic influences. You will never see me celebrate Halloween or drive by my house and see a skeleton or ghost outside my house.

---

102. Mark 5:8

The Bible says, give no place to the enemy.[103] Don't rent a room to guilt, condemnation, or bitterness in your mind any longer.

What's that mean?

Like Jesus, you can command the enemy to flee in Jesus' name. That enemy might be demonic, but it could also be an attack on your health, finances, or family.

Use the authority Jesus gave you through His Word, Blood, and Name.

You can cast out demons in Jesus' name! Give him an eviction notice.

Relationship over religion

A long time ago, I took my kids along with several of their friends to a special denominational service. I won't say the denomination, but they were very charismatic.

One of the boys wore old jeans and a t-shirt. He had long hair and looked a little raggedy. Casey was then, and still is, a great kid, and he was already saved and believed in Jesus.

It was amazing how many people that night came up to him and tried to cast demons out of him. It was funny in the beginning but became a real turn off.

You can't judge a book by the cover.

What's that mean? The cover of a book may look tattered and worn, but what is inside may be an incredible story. Conversely, the cover can look amazing but the story inside isn't worth reading.

Jesus described it this way to the religious.

"You clean the outside of the cup and dish, but inside they are full of greed and self-indulgence. First clean the inside of the cup and dish, and then the outside also will be clean."[104]

---

103. *Ephesians 4:27*
104. *Matthew 23:25*

"In the same way, on the outside you can appear to people as righteous but on the inside, you might be full of hypocrisy and wickedness."[105]

Some churches think you need to make a big scene when you repent and show remorse. If you aren't emotional about it then it must not be true repentance. We don't know what is going on in people's hearts.

When we judge by external responses, we start to drive certain behaviors. People will act a certain way because they know that's what is expected.

I know a woman who would get very passionate in her arguments. If you didn't respond with the same excitement, she thought you were lying or didn't care.

I am naturally calm and reserved. My family never argued. I don't get all worked up over situations. I learned to raise my voice and emotionally respond just to make her believe it was important to me. But that was a learned behavior and not the truth. My lack of emotion didn't mean I didn't care.

People respond differently. And it's ok. You have to give people room to be different. You can't judge them based on your perception alone.

God wants your whole heart. He wants you to come to Him just the way you are. He doesn't want you to pretend or put on a certain mask.

He's not looking for perfection. In fact, none of us are perfect except Jesus. One day when Jesus comes back, we will be perfect. But until that day happens, just keep being your best, improving, being open with God, and seeking after Him.

That's what David did. He wasn't perfect, but He was honest with God.

---

105. *Matthew 23:28*

A man after God's own heart

After King Saul messed up and God took the Kingdom from him, the Prophet Samuel said the Kingdom was being given to someone else - a man after His own heart.[106]

Then when Samuel went to anoint the new King, he went to Jesse's house and met with his son's, God denied them all.

1 Samuel 16:7 says,

"But the LORD said to Samuel, do not consider his appearance or his height, for I have rejected him. The LORD does not look at the things people look at. People look at the outward appearance, but the LORD looks at the heart."

My mother-in-law asked how David could be a man after God's own heart when he committed adultery and then killed the woman's husband.

How many of you have done something wrong? Aren't you glad you God knows your heart and still accepts you! You may mess up, but God still sees your heart.[106]

David was tempted and strayed from God. But when he was confronted about his sins by the Prophet Nathan, he immediately repented.

There were still human consequences over it. He lost a son in the process.

Psalm 32:3-5 says,

> When I kept silent, my bones wasted away through
> my groaning all day long.
>
> For day and night your hand was heavy on me;
> my strength was sapped as in the heat of summer.
>
> Then I acknowledged my sin to you and did not
> cover up my iniquity. I said, "I will confess my

---

106. *1 Samuel 13:14*

transgressions to the LORD." And you forgave the guilt of my sin.

But David responded to God with,

"Create in me a pure heart, O God, and renew a steadfast spirit within me. Do not cast me from your presence or take your Holy Spirit from me. Restore to me the joy of your salvation and grant me a willing spirit, to sustain me."[107]

Self-examination

Self-examination opens us to the love we seek.

David responded,

> "Search me, O God, and know my heart. test me and know my anxious thoughts. Point out anything in me that offends you, and lead me along the path of everlasting life."
>
> Psalms 139: 23-24 NLT

Notice in this version, David asks God to "point out" anything that offends God. What made David a man after God's own heart? It's not that he didn't mess up. But when his mistakes were pointed out to him, he quickly took responsibility and self-corrected.

"The real issue with self-examination isn't that I am inviting God to know me (Since He already does) but that I am inviting God to help me know me."[108]

Here's the Key:

Quickly open your heart to God, seek His forgiveness, turn back to Him by changing your direction.

---

107. *Psalm 51:10-12*
108. *Sacred Rhythms, Ruth Haley Barton, 2006*

Pride comes before the fall

The problem occurs when we become prideful. When we are prideful, we aren't open to feedback. We aren't open to self-evaluation because we are protecting ourselves.

Here's what the Bible says about Pride:

"Pride goes before destruction, a haughty spirit before a fall."[109]

"Humble yourselves, therefore, under God's mighty hand, that he may lift you up in due time."[110]

James said, But He gives us more grace. That is why Scripture says:

"God opposes the proud but shows favor to the humble."

"Submit yourselves, then, to God. Resist the devil, and he will flee from you. Come near to God and he will come near to you. Wash your hands, you sinners, and purify your hearts, you doubleminded."[111]

Be aware

The enemy doesn't give up. When Jesus fasted for forty days in the desert and the devil tried to entice Him, He used God's Word against His own son. But Jesus responded in kind with the Word of God.

Then in the amplified version says, When the devil had finished every temptation, he [temporarily] left Him until a more opportune time.

Our enemy is always looking for a more opportune time so be on the lookout. The good news is you already have the victory through Jesus. So even if you fall, get back up and keep going.

9-1-1 What's Your Emergency?

To me, Psalms 91 is the "go to" scripture when it comes to emergencies.

If you don't know what to pray, dial Psalms 91:1 . . .

---

109. *Proverbs 16:18*
110. *1 Peter 5:6*
111. *James 4:6-8*

PSALMS 91

Whoever dwells in the shelter of the Most-High will rest in the shadow of the Almighty.

He will say of the LORD, "He is my refuge and my fortress, my God, in whom I trust."

Surely, he will save you from the fowler's snare and from the deadly pestilence. He will cover you with his feathers, and under his wings you will find refuge; his faithfulness will be your shield and rampart. You will not fear the terror of night, nor the arrow that flies by day, nor the pestilence that stalks in the darkness, nor the plague that destroys at midday.

A thousand may fall at your side, ten thousand at your right hand, but it will not come near you. You will only observe with your eyes and see the punishment of the wicked.

If you say, "The LORD is my refuge," and you make the Most High your dwelling, no harm will overtake you, no disaster will come near your tent. For he will command his angels concerning you to guard you in all your ways; they will lift you up in their hands, so that you will not strike your foot against a stone.

You will tread on the lion and the cobra; you will trample the great lion and the serpent. "Because he loves me," says the LORD, "I will rescue him; I will protect him, for he acknowledges my name. He will call on me, and I will answer him; I will be with him in trouble, I will deliver him and honor him.

With long life I will satisfy him and show him my salvation.

Chapter Twelve

HIGHER POWER

The first big leadership assignment I had at Lakewood Church was overseeing the Prayer Partners. At the time, there were something like 800 prayer volunteers.

One of the amazing things about both John and Joel Osteen is they've included individual prayer time for people during most every service. People can come up front and receive one-on-one prayer for their personal needs.

Over time, I saw some patterns in what people were asking to receive prayer for.

As I trained and orientated new prayer partners, I would encourage them that if they learned scriptures around these frequent prayer requests, they could pray for anyone.

The initial concern for new prayer partners was that they wouldn't know what to pray for someone. This would put them more at ease. I've also seen recently that when I ask people to become new leaders, their biggest hesitation is "I don't pray like you do".

The good news is prayer is highly trainable. The disciples asked Jesus to teach them to pray.

Jesus' teaching on prayer

One day Jesus was praying in a certain place. When he finished, one of his disciples said to him, Lord, teach us to pray.

He said to them, when you pray, say:

> "Father, hallowed be your name, your kingdom come.
> Give us each day our daily bread. Forgive us our sins,
> for we also forgive everyone who sins against us. And
> lead us not into temptation."
>
> Luke 11:2-4

The annoying friend[112]

Jesus goes on to share a story. It was about an annoying friend who knocks on your door late at night. You don't want to get out of bed but because of his incessant knocking you finally do.

I love what Jesus says, I tell you, even though he will not get up and give you the bread because of friendship, yet because of your shameless audacity he will surely get up and give you as much as you need.

Have you reached the point of shameless audacity?

Persistent widow[113]

Jesus also shares how there was a widow who kept going to the judge saying things were unfair. She wouldn't take no for an answer but kept expressing that things were unfair!

The judge kept saying, "No . . . No . . . No". But because of her persistence. Because she keeps bothering me. Because she won't give up. Because she won't take no for an answer.

Because of what Jesus did for us and reconciled us with God, we can now go directly to God with our requests.

Jesus also knows what it was like to be tempted, to struggle with the flesh, to go hungry. He experienced loss and experienced compassion for people's issues. It's not like we are praying to a God who doesn't understand what it is like to be human.

---

112. *Luke 11:8*
113. *Luke 18:1-8*

> "Let us then approach God's throne of grace with
> confidence, so that we may receive mercy and find grace
> to help us in our time of need."
>
> Hebrews 4:16

How badly do you want it?

Based on what Jesus said about prayer, I would ask you, how bad do you want your miracle? How bad do you want things to change? Are you willing to bug God? Are you willing to keep asking, seeking, knocking, pursuing, not quitting, not giving in, not giving up?

I like receiving the doctors' reports from people. That way, I know specifically what to pray for.

Pray specifically for what you and others need.

Do you want to get well?

Jesus asked a disabled man who had been stuck in the same place for 38 years, do you want to get well?

What a question! How long have you been stuck in your situation? Has it become attached to your identity? Do you want to get well, or do you want to stay where you are? How bad do you want to get healed?

Praying God's Will

God's Word is His Will. When we know what He's promised us, we can pray His word with confidence.

For instance, we don't have to pray, God, if it is your will heal me. We know that it is His will to heal you. So instead, we can pray, God, Your Word says, by the stripes of Jesus I am healed. So right now, I thank you that I am healed in Jesus' name.

Common prayer requests

Do you want to know what those common prayer requests are?

I am including some scriptures along with them so you can pray for yourself, friends, family and others who may be going through something right now and in the future.

1. Financial / Job Struggles

But remember the LORD your God, for it is he who gives you the ability to produce wealth, and so confirms his covenant, which he swore to your ancestors, as it is today.[114]

Bring the whole tithe into the storehouse, so that there may be food in my house. Test me in this, says the LORD Almighty, and see if I will not throw open the floodgates of heaven and pour out so much blessing that there will not be room enough to store it.[115]

A good person leaves an inheritance for their children's children, but a sinner's wealth is stored up for the righteous.[116]

Sample Prayer: Lord, you say that I am blessed to be a blessing, that you give us the wisdom to get wealth. I thank you for blessing my brother or sister right now and helping them to live an abundant life. I speak a job into existence right now in Jesus' name and ask for divine connections. That employers will be chasing him or her down in Jesus' name.

2. Health Issues

"He himself bore our sins in his body on the cross, so that we might die to sins and live for righteousness; by his wounds you have been healed."[117]

---

114. Deuteronomy 8:18
115. Malachi 3:10
116. Proverbs 13:22
117. Psalm 103:2-4

"With long life I will satisfy him and show him my salvation"

Psalm 91:16

"Praise the LORD, my soul, and forget not all his benefits—who forgives all your sins and heals all your diseases, who redeems your life from the pit and crowns you with love and compassion."[118]

Sample Prayer: Lord, I believe you are my healer. You say, by the stripes of Jesus I am healed. So right now, I command this sickness to leave my body and loose your angels to fight this battle for me, In Jesus name.

3. Marriage and Relationships

Haven't you read, he (Jesus) replied, that at the beginning the Creator made them male and female, and said, 'For this reason a man will leave his father and mother and be united to his wife, and the two will become one flesh'? So, they are no longer two, but one flesh. Therefore, what God has joined together, let no one separate.[119]

"He who finds a wife finds what is good and receives favor from the LORD."[120]

Sample Prayer: Lord, you say that he who finds a wife finds a good thing. You say the two will become one. You said it's only because of our hardness of hearts that Moses granted a certificate of divorce. So, I ask you to soften our hearts, bring forgiveness and bring unity to our house in Jesus' name.

4. Mental Health and Coping Mechanisms

"So if the Son sets you free, you will be free indeed."[121]

118.
119. *Matthew 19:4-6*
120. *Proverbs 18:22*
121. *John 8:36*

"The thief comes only to steal and kill and destroy; I have come that they may have life and have it to the full."[122]

Sample Prayer: Lord, you say that He who the son sets free is free indeed. I thank you right now that I am free from depression, free from anxiety, free from addiction, In the name of Jesus. I bind the devil and demon forces that have come to kill, still and destroy. You came to give me life. Thank you for setting me free.

5. Salvation for Family Members
"As for me and my household, we will serve the LORD."[123]

People often pray for the salvation of their family and friends, asking God to soften hearts and draw them closer to Him.

Salvation is a deep spiritual need, and prayer plays a crucial role in interceding for those we love. We can pray for God to reveal Himself and bring them to a saving knowledge of Jesus Christ.

Sample Prayer: Lord, I lift my loved one to You. I ask that You soften their heart and open their eyes to Your truth. May they come to know You personally and receive the gift of salvation. I trust You to work in their life, in Jesus' name, Amen.

Specific Prayers

Here are some specific prayers around situations you or someone you know may be dealing with or know someone who is dealing with. Pray specifically for your needs or the needs of others in Jesus' name.

Addiction

Addiction is a powerful force that can take control of your life, pulling you away from the fullness of God's plan for you. Whether it's substance abuse, unhealthy habits, or any other form of dependency, God's desire is for you

---

122. John 10:10
123. Joshua 24:15

to be free. He wants to break the chains of addiction, restore your mind, body, and spirit, and guide you to a life of freedom and fulfillment in Him.

Prayer: Lord, I thank you that you came to give me life to the fullest. I ask you to break the chains that have held me down. Take this addiction from me and give me the strength to stay on the best path for my life. I cast this care on you because you care for me. In Jesus name.

Anger

Anger can be a natural response to hurt or injustice, but when it becomes overwhelming or uncontrolled, it can disrupt our relationships and hinder our spiritual growth. God calls us to live in peace, and through His love and healing, He can remove the root of anger. By forgiving those who have hurt us and allowing God to soften our hearts, we can experience His peace and freedom.

Prayer: I know you are a Good God. You are full of unconditional love. I ask you to search my heart and take away the root of my anger. I forgive anyone who hurt me and the bitterness that has held me back. Soften my heart and heal me completely. I thank you that I am free from Anger and will live a life that honors you and brings joy to others in Jesus' name.

Anxiety

Anxiety can overwhelm us, causing fear and uncertainty about the future. However, God's Word tells us not to worry, but to trust Him in all things. He promises a peace that surpasses all understanding, one that guards our hearts and minds. In the midst of anxiety, we can lean on His faithfulness and find rest in His presence.

Prayer: Lord, you say to be anxious for nothing, so right now I ask you for the peace of God that surpasses all understanding. Thank you for freeing me in Jesus' name.

Cancer

Cancer can bring fear and uncertainty, but God's healing power is greater than any diagnosis. Through Jesus' sacrifice on the cross, we have access to divine healing. No matter the severity of the condition, God's Word tells us that by His stripes we are healed. Through faith and prayer, we can trust God to restore our bodies and bring complete healing.

Prayer: Cancer, I command you to flee my body now in the name of Jesus. I command any sickness or disease to leave me at this very hour and confess your word that says, by the stripes of Jesus I am healed. I loose your Angels to bring it to pass. With long life you will satisfy me and show me your salvation.

Codependency and Unhealthy Relationships
(See Chapter 18: No Judgement Zone)

Codependency often leads us to seek validation and identity through others, especially in unhealthy relationships. God created you to be whole and complete in Him, and He wants to heal your heart and restore your sense of self-worth. By renewing your identity in Christ, you can break free from the chains of unhealthy attachments and trust God to bring the right people into your life.

Prayer: Lord, I know that I am a Child of the Most-High God. I know that you love me. Heal my heart and build up my self-esteem. Transform my identity and self-image to reflect you. Protect me from the wrong relationships and bring the right people into my life in Jesus' name.

Crisis

When facing challenging or uncertain circumstances, people often seek peace and calm in the middle of their storms, trusting that God will provide stability and hope.

Storms in life - whether financial, relational, or health-related - can be overwhelming. Prayer brings peace and helps us trust in God's faithfulness even during crises.

Prayer: Lord, I am facing a storm right now, but I know you are with me. Please give me peace amid this trial and help me to trust You with all my heart. Calm my fears and remind me of Your promises that You will never leave me. In Jesus' name, Amen.

Cutting

Why do people cut themselves? Cutting and self-harm are often a desperate attempt to regain control over overwhelming emotions. It might provide you with temporary relief from the pain you feel inside.

It's a painful expression of deeper inner struggles, but God offers hope and healing. He understands your pain and is ready to help you find freedom and peace. Surrendering your struggles to Him can bring healing and restore the peace that only He can provide.

Prayer: Lord, I need your help. My life is out of control, and I can't handle it on my own. I surrender my life to you right now and ask for your help in overcoming this issue. I need you to heal me in Jesus' name.

Depression and/or Suicidal Ideation

Depression is complex. Some people go through times of depression around circumstances and others have more severe depression involving medication.

While I hope that you will be set free from any dependence on medication, sometimes it is needed to correct our chemistry.

Prayer: We come against depression in the name of Jesus. We ask you to take that depression from me and fill me with your joy.

I come against wrong thoughts and thoughts of suicide in the name of Jesus and take those thoughts captive. I thank You that I am a Child of God, created in Your image. Thank you for freeing me and that I have the mind of Christ, in Jesus' name.

Diabetes

Diabetes is a chronic condition that affects your body's ability to manage blood sugar levels. It can be a challenge, but God is able to bring healing and restoration to every part of your body. He promises to give you wisdom to care for your health, and His desire is for you to experience wholeness and vitality. With faith, you can trust God to work in your body for complete healing.

Prayer: Lord, I command that diabetes to leave my body now in Jesus' name. I bind the devil and demon forces that have come to kill, steal and destroy, and loose your Angels to bring it to pass. Thank you for healing me. Thank you that everything within my body functions into perfection. Help me to eat the right things and not the wrong things. Thank you for a long, healthy life, in Jesus' name.

Divorce

Jesus said it is because of our hardness of hearts that God granted a certificate of divorce. You don't want to pass it down generationally.

Divorce happens but we want to heal from it and learn from it so we don't repeat it over and over again.

Divorce can leave emotional scars and deep pain, especially when it affects families. Though divorce is a reality in our broken world, God desires healing, restoration, and reconciliation. He wants to soften your heart and heal your wounds so that you can move forward in peace. God also promises to break generational cycles of divorce and dysfunction, bringing freedom to your life and family.

Prayer: God, I ask you to soften my heart. I want to be completely healed from the inside out. Take away my insecurities and hurt. I break any generational curses and thank you for breaking this from my life and bloodline in Jesus' name. I release it to you!

Domestic Abuse

1 in 4 women and 1 in 9 men in the U.S. have experienced severe intimate partner physical violence, sexual violence, or stalking in their lifetime.[124]

On average, 20 people per minute are physically abused by an intimate partner in the U.S.[125]

Prayer: God, you know what I've experienced. Someone I should have been able to trust hurt me. I release the trauma to you and ask you to take it from me. Help me to heal and trust others. Protect me from the wrong people and surround me with the right people. I ask for your help, in Jesus' name.

Fear

There is healthy fear and unhealthy fear. When we are in danger, fear launches our natural fight, flight or freeze instinct.

However, when our fears work against us and disrupt our lives, it can cause more harm than good.

Prayer: God, you didn't give me a spirit of fear but of power and love and of sound mind. I bind that spirit of fear in my life in Jesus' name and I thank you that I am free from fear. I lose your power in my life. Give me the strength and Boldness to do Your Will and fulfill my destiny in Jesus' name.

Generational Curses

(See Chapter 11: From Prey to Pray)

Generational curses refer to patterns of negative behavior or afflictions that pass from one generation to the next. These can include issues such as addiction, poverty, or sickness. The good news is that through Jesus, we have a new bloodline. He came to break the cycle of dysfunction and

---

124. CDC, *National Intimate Partner and Sexual Violence Survey*
125. *National Coalition Against Domestic Violence – NCADV*

bring freedom to us and our families. By faith, we can break these curses and walk in the fullness of God's blessings.

Prayer: I plead the blood of Jesus over my household and thank You Lord that any evil must pass over us. I bind the devil and demon forces that would come to kill steel and destroy in Jesus' name and loose your angels to fight every battle for me. I break any generational curse from my family now and thank you Jesus there is no more addiction, poverty, or sickness in my life in Jesus' name. Bless us for generations to come.

Grief

Grief is a natural process to help us with the loss of someone or something. We all deal with loss differently. There is no set way or length of time for grieving. The important thing is to get help if you need it and allow yourself to grieve and to heal.

You may experience some level of anger and depression. This is normal. It is only an issue if you get stuck and can't move forward. Give yourself time to get well.

(There are also grief support classes available for you).

Prayer: Lord, I am struggling with losing _____. I ask for your help to heal my heart. I look to You because You are where my help comes from. It is hard to be without them. Thank you for your complete healing and helping me through this process, in Jesus' name.

Homosexuality

God created man and woman in His image. He said they should come together and become one. They should be fruitful and multiply.

Marriage between a man and a woman is God's design. Anything else is a counterfeit. The intimacy of marriage is a display of Jesus and the Church. The Groom and the Bride.

I also have found through experience that some people have been molested as children. Many times, it was by people who should have taken care of them. It can challenge our identity. If that happened to you, I am truly sorry.

Prayer: God, I want to follow your design. I ask you to break anything that doesn't come from you out of my life. I command that spirit of homosexuality to flee in the name of Jesus.

I forgive anyone or _____ specifically and release them to you and ask you to cleanse me. I break the struggle with homosexuality from my life and lose your angels to fight this battle for me and bring it to pass in Jesus' name.

Mental Health and Mental Illness

Mental health issues can range from temporary struggles to more severe conditions. Whether caused by trauma, genetic factors, or environmental stress, mental health challenges are real and need to be addressed. God's desire is for us to be whole, and prayer can invite healing into our minds and hearts.

Through prayer, we can ask for God's peace, restoration of our minds, and healing from the effects of trauma and illness. Trusting in God's ability to heal every area of our lives helps us find hope.

Prayer: Jesus, you came to set me totally free. I ask you to heal me completely. I confess that I am in my right mind and have the mind of Christ. Cause my brain and brain chemistry to be in perfect alignment so that I won't struggle with mental illness anymore. Heal me from any genetic, traumatic, social, environmental or physical causes. I surrender to you and thank You for making me well, In Jesus' Name!

Oppression or Possession
(See Chapter 11: From Prey to Pray)

There are demonic forces at work in the world. This came from the prideful fall of Lucifer and a third of the angels from heaven. He is called by many names like the devil, the father of lies, prince of darkness, accuser, deceiver, Beelzebub, and the anti-Christ.

The Bible says that people can open the door to spiritual forces through witchcraft or being part of the occult. King Saul was being tormented so he had a witch bring the ghost of Samuel back from the dead. This is something the law forbids but he did it anyway.

James 4:7 says, "Submit yourselves, then, to God. Resist the devil, and he will flee from you."

Prayer: Lord, I repent of all demonic activity I have been involved in. I also ask forgiveness for the sins of my fathers and to break any generational curses in my bloodline. I plead the blood of Jesus over my life and thank you for setting me free. I command you Satan to get your hands off me now in Jesus' name. Get out of my life. I confess Jesus is my Lord and Savior.

Pornography and Sexual Perversion

Pornography and sexual perversion can distort our understanding of love and relationships. These struggles often stem from unhealthy desires and may be rooted in past wounds or unaddressed needs.

Approximately 1 million people are watching online pornography every minute. 46% of men and 16% of women in the U.S. consume porn regularly. Teens and young adults say "not recycling" is more immoral than viewing porn. About 7.7 million Americans struggle with pornography addiction.[126]

Prayer helps us surrender these desires to God, seeking His healing and transformation. By asking for God's forgiveness, cleansing, and strength,

---

126. *Maze of Love, Porn Statistics, 2024*

we can break free from the grip of sexual sin and walk in purity and honor in our relationships.

Prayer: God, you say not to look at people in lust. Forgive me for the sins I have committed with my eyes and my flesh. Take any wrong desires from me. Heal my heart and wash me clean. I want to honor you with my Body. I turn from it now and seek after You, in Jesus' name.

Prejudice and Social Injustices

Prejudice, whether based on race, class, or other differences, is a sin that creates division among people.

As Christians, we are called to love our neighbors, no matter their background. Through prayer, we can ask God to heal our hearts and minds from any biases or prejudices we may hold. We can also seek God's guidance in fighting for justice and equality for all people, reflecting God's love and compassion in everything we do.

There are all kinds of prejudices and injustices in the world. We judge people we don't understand. We aren't born prejudiced, but we can learn to hate or dislike others based on certain characteristics.

Prayer: God, I know we were all created in your image, and you love us all equally. Through Jesus, there are no more divisions because of race, gender, color of skin or other differences. We are all one in Christ. I ask you now to renew my mind and take away any wrong thinking, prejudice against others, biases, economic or social status, and wrong teachings and experiences in Jesus' name. Let prejudice in my family stop with me and that my children and their children are free right now. Forgive me for any negative impact I might have had on others and open my eyes to the injustices you want me to care about. Help me to love all people the way you love them, in Jesus' name.

Selfishness and Selfish Ambitions

We were born selfish. Without Jesus, we all have a level of selfishness and selfish ambitions. We might use lies and manipulation to get what we want. We can also use people for our own needs and desires without really caring about them. We can also attack others verbally to protect our egos. Even in marriage, we can try to control our spouse and seek our own desires above theirs.

The good news is when we give our lives to Jesus and receive the Holy Spirit, He starts to change us. We can start to care for others and love unconditionally.

Prayer: Lord, I have been selfish and sought my own desires. I struggle with loving others the way you love them. I want to be unselfish and love unconditionally. Free me from my flesh and guide me by your spirit. I bind my flesh and ask your spirit to change me. I surrender the need for control to you. Thank you for setting me free, in Jesus' name.

Trauma and PTSD

About 70% of adults in the U.S. have experienced at least one traumatic event in their lives — that's approximately 223 million people.[127]

1 in 5 people who experience a traumatic event will develop PTSD.[128]

If you've experienced trauma, you are not alone. Most people have faced painful or overwhelming moments at some point in their lives.

For some, trauma may have stretched over months or even years. No matter your story, know this: there is hope. Healing is possible. Through connection with safe, trustworthy people, your brain can begin to rewire, and your body can learn to feel calm again.

Prayer: Lord, thank you for loving me. I have been impacted by trauma and need your help to heal. Please bring trustworthy people into my life and help me overcome the impact and residual effects of my experiences.

---

127. National Council for Mental Wellbeing
128. U.S. Department of Veterans Affairs

Thank you for connecting me with the right people and protecting me from the wrong influences. I thank you that I am whole, in Jesus' name.

Unforgiveness
(See Chapter 15: Fly Free)

Jesus told us to forgive. If we don't, how can God forgive us? You can forgive before you feel it. You aren't letting them off the hook. You are freeing yourself.

John 20:23 says, "If you forgive anyone's sins, their sins are forgiven; if you do not forgive them, they are not forgiven."

Prayer: God, I thank you for loving me so much that you sent your son Jesus to die for me. You forgave me from my sins. Because you forgave me to the extreme, by faith I forgive the person or people who hurt me. Heal my heart. Set me free. I release any bitterness or judgment to you in Jesus' name.

Chapter Thirteen

AN ATTITUDE OF GRATITUDE

My good friend Jason shared a story that I thought made a great point around being thankful. There once was a man who was with a group of friends, and he told them a joke, and everyone laughed uncontrollably.

After a few minutes the man told the same joke, he got some laughter, but it was mostly just smiled. He told the joke again for a third time, but this time no one was laughing. The man asked, "why isn't anyone laughing?" and someone from the group said, "you've told the same exact joke three times, it's not funny anymore." The man answered, "If you can't laugh at the same joke over and over again, why are you always complaining about the same problems over and over again expecting things to change?" We need to turn our complaints into thankfulness, because in the same way telling a joke repeatedly gets old, so does complaining.

There are things in your control and things out of your control. You can't control the weather, the traffic, or how your family acts on holidays. Complaining about things you can't change is a waste of time. And usually complaining about them doesn't make you feel any better.

The best way to shift your attitude is to appreciate yourself and what you have.

I'd like to share a few things that I had to do to shift my way of thinking, and I pray that you can apply it to your life.

Being grateful

"Gratitude follows grace and prepares the heart for more grace still."[129]

Philippians 4:11-12 (NLT) says,

"Not that I was ever in need, for I have learned to be content with whatever I have. I know how to live on almost nothing or everything. I have learned the secret of living in every situation, whether it is with a full stomach or empty, with plenty or little."

This verse was written by the Apostle Paul while he was in a prison cell. Talk about having a grateful spirit…this man had contentment down.

So often, we take the things we have in life for granted.

- *Our Jobs.* We have a way to provide for our family, and instead of giving thanks we complain about having to work (and some of you may have prayed and fasted to be where you are now, God opened a door and now you're complaining about it).
- *Our Car.* We don't have that new shiny car, fully loaded, but hey, you have something that gets you from point A to point B – you don't have to rely on anyone else
- *Our Homes.* Maybe it's not the biggest house in the world, or maybe you live in an apartment wishing you had a house, but you have a roof over your head – you could be living on the street

The Three "C"s

Being grateful shifts us from the three "C"s of Comparison, Criticism, and Complaining.

The easiest way to miss out on the promises and blessings God has for your life is by complaining – just ask the Israelites.

Then the Lord said to Moses and Aaron, how long must I put up with this wicked community and its complaints about me? Yes, I have heard the

---

129. *N.T. Wright, New Testament Scholar, University of Oxford*

complaints the Israelites are making against me. Now tell them this: 'As surely as I live, declares the Lord, I will do to you the very things I heard you say. You will all drop dead in this wilderness! Because you complained against me.

What are you complaining about? The Israelites knew how to complain. God used plagues to save the Israelites from Egyptian oppression, He parted the Red Sea so they could walk on dry ground, He provided manna and quail for food, He met their every need…yet, when they were right on the cusp of entering the promised land, they grumbled and complained. Because of this they missed out on the promised land, and tonight I'm wondering – what is it that you are complaining, or grumbling about that's causing you to miss out on God's promises[130]?

A great challenge would be to intentionally replace every complaint with a moment of gratitude. Instead of saying, *"I wish I had…"*, we could say, *"I'm thankful that God has already provided…"* It's amazing how perspective shifts when we focus on God's faithfulness rather than our frustrations.

What's an area in your life where you feel God is calling you to shift from complaining to gratitude?

God created you special!

> "Comparison is the thief of joy."
>
> Teddy Roosevelt

Pay careful attention to your own work, for then you will get the satisfaction of a job well done, and you won't need to compare yourself to anyone else[131].

It's difficult at first to not compare. Especially with social media. It's made it so easy for us to fall into this trap - I'm certainly guilty of this. It's

---

130. *Numbers 14:26-30 (NLT)*
131. *Galatians 6:4*

easy to see a post of someone's vacation, their new promotion at work, their family and say things like, "why can't that be me?" That's why research is starting to show a correlation with anxiety and depression in people who use social media heavily – and believe me, I'm not against using social media. I use it myself. But try to limit your intake – otherwise you may fall victim to this trap of comparison.[132]

You'll start seeing all these amazing things occurring in the lives of other people and start believing that nothing good is happening for you.

Remember that social media is not a complete picture of life. No one's on Instagram posting their failures or struggles – and trust me - we all struggle with something – so don't go believing that someone's life is better than yours just because of what they post on social media. So, stop making comparisons, they'll steal your joy and make you lose sight of all the blessings in your life.

When you believe in yourself, you have no reason to complain because you understand that, although life will never be completely fair, God has equipped you with everything you need to be who He called you to be.

Do you criticize others? Have others criticized you? There are plenty of critics in the world. I have always admired the way Joel Osteen doesn't respond to his critics. He lets it go in one ear and out the other.

Many times, people who criticize are jealous or maybe making assumptions about you that may or may not be true. God wants us to build each other up, not tear each other down.

If you want to be hard to offend, you must start filtering out the negative and not responding to those who criticize you. I know it's not easy, but it will bring more peace into your life.

It's also why we make those declarations we read about in an earlier chapter. It's not just "good vibes". Sometimes we need those reminders, we need to remember how God sees us. And maybe today you don't feel

---

132. *Journal of Social and Clinical Psychology,* 2018

like any of those things – you don't feel blessed, prosperous, redeemed, forgiven, talented, or creative – but guess what, God says you are all of this and more! Believe in yourself the way God believes in you. You are enough because God says you are enough.

God says you are well able. He says you are blessed and highly favored, He says you are head and not the tail, He says you are above and not beneath, He calls you mighty in the land!

Laugh along the way

Take time to laugh. Call a funny friend, watch a comedy, or check out cute videos online. Laughter reduces anxiety and depression. That's one of the reasons Joel Osteen starts every message with a joke. It gets us in the right frame of mind.

A joyful heart is good medicine, but a crushed spirit dries up the bones.[133]

And don't take yourself too seriously! We are all a work in progress. We don't know everything even if we think we do, and we all do funny things sometimes. It's ok to laugh at yourself!

WHAT ARE YOU THANKFUL FOR?

You can be happy now

Don't put it off!

Have you ever said "When I _____ I will be happy . . ."

When I have money ...

When I get married ...

When I retire ...

Wouldn't you rather choose to be happy than sad? You can choose to be happy now. Don't wait to be happy when you can be happy now.

---

133. *Proverbs 17:22*

Do you want to be happy? Gratitude has been proven to be linked to happiness.

Overflow

God says You will overflow with thankfulness.

"And now, just as you accepted Christ Jesus as your Lord, you must continue to follow him. Let your roots grow down into him, and let your lives be built on him. Then your faith will grow strong in the truth you were taught, and you will *overflow* with thankfulness."[134]

If you focus on Jesus, your roots will grow deep, THEN your faith will grow strong, and you will overflow. He is the God of the overflow.

This is why we put sitting at the feet of Jesus as the most important way to start your day. If you will spend time with God in the morning, then you will overflow with the rest. Put first things first. What do you need to do to shift your perspective? Think of good things. Think about what you have and not what you don't.

GRATITUDE IS A KEY TO FREEDOM

Create a Thankfulness List[135]

There are so many things we can complain about, but this exercise allows you to remind yourself of how blessed you really are?

Did you know that being grateful is not only good for you spiritually, but it also has been proven to be beneficial to your health. A study done by University of California San Diego's School of Medicine found that

---

134. Colossians 2:6-7 (NLT)
135. Peter 2:24

people who are more grateful have better heart health, lower blood pressure, improved immunity and better sleep.

Even the Bible encourages us to keep a positive attitude.

> "Rejoice always, pray continually, give thanks in all circumstances; for this is God's will for you in Christ Jesus."
> 1 Thessalonians 5:16-18

It doesn't say give thanks FOR all circumstances. It says, … give thanks in all circumstances . . .

This doesn't mean ignoring your problems but believing that despite what you are facing God will make a way. Your circumstances may not be good but focus on what God says about your situation.

You do this by saying,

Lord, I know I have this illness, but I know that "by Your stripes I am healed."[135]

I know the situation I'm facing right now hurts, but you work all things out for my good.

Lord my heart was broken, but I am thankful that you heal the broken hearted."[136]

This financial situation looks impossible, but You are Jehovah-Jireh – My Provider[137]. I am blessed to be a blessing!

Although depression makes me feel like I'm all alone, I know that you are with me and even though I walk through the darkest valley, I will fear no evil, for you are with me.[138]

When you start thanking God for what you have and stop focusing on what you don't, you'll be more satisfied, you'll walk with confidence, and God will be able to trust you with more.

---

136. Psalm 34:18
137. Genesis 22:4
138. Psalm 23:4

Freedom challenge

We are going to do just that; we are going to create a list of the things we are thankful for.

For at least the next 30 days, I want to encourage you to go over this list at the beginning of each day. You can even add to the list as you think of more things you are thankful for *(Use the Gratitude List Template provided).*

As you go over your list each day, take a moment to really reflect on the blessings you have. How does focusing on gratitude shift your perspective and mindset? Notice how your thoughts and emotions change over time.

Each week, try focusing on a different area of life. For example, one week might be about relationships, another about work, and another about personal growth. This will help you see gratitude in all

GRATITUDE LIST TEMPLATE

What are you thankful for? Try to thank God for 3 things each day.

GRATITUDE LIST (EXAMPLE)

God, thank you for . . .
1. Giving me air to breath
2. Waking me up this morning
3. Giving me food to eat
4. Water to drink
5. A roof over my head
6. A job
7. Giving me life
8. Health
9. Providing for my needs
10. Creating me
11. Saving me
12. Giving me gifts, talents and abilities
13. Strength for today
14. Friends and family
15. A church family
16. A place to lay my head at night
17. A wife or husband
18. Children
19. A future and a hope . . .

Chapter Fourteen

LETTING GO OF THE PAST

We've all had disappointments - dreams that didn't happen. Maybe someone hurt you, left you, or broke your heart. Maybe you faced rejection or loss. Letting go of the past is one of the hardest things we're asked to do. But you know what's harder? Staying stuck.

The Israelites wandered in the wilderness for forty years - not because God wasn't willing to lead them into the Promised Land, but because they couldn't let go of their past. They longed to go back to Egypt, back to slavery, because they didn't have the faith to move forward. If they had just let go, they might have entered into all God had for them.

Don't die in the desert of your past. Right across the Jordan River is your promised land—a land filled with blessing, abundance, and freedom.

As the Apostle Paul reminds us:

> "Brothers and sisters, I do not consider myself yet to have taken hold of it. But one thing I do: Forgetting what is behind and straining toward what is ahead, I press on toward the goal to win the prize for which God has called me heavenward in Christ Jesus."
>
> Philippians 3:13-14

Failing Forward

Mistakes aren't mistakes if you learn from them. Every struggle, every setback is an opportunity to grow. God uses even our failures to strengthen our character.

Thomas Edison is often said to have made over 1,000 attempts before perfecting the light bulb. Whether or not that number is exact, the point is clear: each failure brought him one step closer to success.

He once said, "Many of life's failures are people who did not realize how close they were to success when they gave up."

Failure isn't final. Abraham Lincoln once said, "Always bear in mind that your own resolution to succeed is more important than any other one thing." And Albert Einstein remarked, "A person who never made a mistake never tried anything new."

Vince Lombardi said it simply: *"It's not whether you get knocked down; it's whether you get up."*

Leadership expert John Maxwell calls this mindset "failing forward." He writes:

"The difference between average people and achieving people is their perception of and response to failure."

The Bible says:

"For though the righteous fall seven times, they rise again, but the wicked stumble when calamity strikes."[139]

"Many are the afflictions of the righteous, but the Lord delivers him out of them all."[140]

Discipline and Growth

Children are hard-wired for struggle. Letting them fail in safe ways helps them grow. God does the same with us. His discipline is never to harm us - it's to shape us into who He created us to be.

Hebrews 12:5-11 reminds us:

"My son, do not make light of the Lord's discipline... the Lord disciplines the one He loves."

---

139. Proverbs 24:16
140. Psalm 34:19

"Endure hardship as discipline... God disciplines us for our good, in order that we may share in His holiness."

It may not feel good in the moment, but it produces a harvest of righteousness and peace.

Nothing Is Wasted

Romans 8:28 says:

"And we know that in all things God works for the good of those who love Him, who have been called according to His purpose."

God doesn't waste a thing. Your pain, your regrets, your darkest moments - they all have a purpose in God's greater plan.

The Power of Resilience

Resilience isn't just surviving hard times. It's about growing stronger through them.

Olympic gymnasts learn this early. Gymnast Shelby McNamara shared how her coaches wouldn't let her stop mid-routine after a mistake. She had to keep going. That kind of persistence built mental strength.

Nina Sossamon Pogue says:

"The definition of resilience is adapting positively to whatever happens in your life and moving forward."

James 1:2-4 reminds us:

"Consider it pure joy, my brothers and sisters, whenever you face trials... because the testing of your faith produces perseverance."

Worship in the Storm

Horatio Spafford lost nearly everything - his business, his son, and his four daughters. Yet on a ship passing over the place where his daughters drowned, he wrote:

"When peace like a river attendeth my way... it is well, it is well with my soul."

His worship amid tragedy still echoes today. You can say, *"It is well with my soul,"* even in your pain.

Romans 5:3-4 says:

"We also rejoice in our sufferings, because we know that suffering produces perseverance; perseverance, character; and character, hope."

Letting go of the weight

In his book *Focus*, J.J. Moses compares holding on to your past to carrying a bag of bricks. It weighs you down and keeps you from moving forward.

Let it go. Release the anger. Forgive the hurt. Trust that God has something better ahead.

Pruned for a Purpose

Jesus said in John 15 that God prunes us so we'll bear more fruit. Pruning is painful - but purposeful. Trust that God is cutting away what's not needed for your future.

Stay connected to Him. That's the key.

Never Give In

Winston Churchill once said:

"Never give in - never, never, never, never—in nothing, great or small... never give in except to convictions of honor and good sense."

Peer pressure doesn't end in adolescence. It shows up in all stages of life. But when you say "no" and mean it, pressure loses its power.

"The devil will give up when he sees that you are not going to give in."

Let it go

God has something better waiting.

You may have made some mistakes in the past. It's time to let it go. Put the past in the past and move forward into your destiny.

No one is perfect, but you are perfectly you.

LETTING GO OF THE PAST IS A KEY TO FREEDOM

Break every chain

There is a heaviness in carrying around the chains of the past. It's hard to let go of the things we've done wrong or the wrongs that have been done to us. "He brought them out of darkness, the utter darkness, and broke away their chains."[141]

What's holding you back?

Many of us spend years feeling like something was literally holding us back. The truth is, we all have "chains" that are meant to slow us down and stop our progress.

There are many chains that try to restrict us:
- **Chains of Guilt** - where we beat ourselves up for past mistakes
- **Chains of Depression** - That dark cloud following us around
- **Chains of Low Self-Esteem** – That makes us think that we're not good enough and makes us feel unlovable

In Acts 12, Peter was thrown in prison after his friend and fellow disciple James was arrested and killed. The Bible clearly says that the church was earnestly praying to God for Peter.

Peter was bound by two chains, then an angel smacked him on the side and said, "get up quickly" and when Peter got up the chains fell off.

The key is to get up quickly!! Don't stay down. Did you notice that

---

141. *Psalms 107:14*

the angel didn't break the chains or unlock them? The most important thing to do when you're bound by chains is "get-up" and get moving in the right direction.

Don't give up or give in because God will break your chains the moment you rise up and take step in the right direction.

Be assured of this, like the church did for Peter, I am praying earnestly for you.

Key Reflection: What's one thing you need to let go of today so you can move forward?

Setting Boundaries: The Soccer Field

When you know what you stand for, it will make it easier to say no to anything that doesn't fit.

In sports, there are boundaries. What boundaries do you need to set?

I liken it to a soccer field. Players know where the boundaries are. The referee will verify what's in and out of bounds.

An example might include:

In bounds: *Attend Bible study each week*

Out of bounds: *Going to the club with acquaintances who drink and discourage you from being more.*

Your response next time they ask you out might be to invite them to the Bible study or church instead. It's then their choice whether or not to go but you've got a made-up mind.

Where do you need to set the boundaries? Do you know where the line is?

IN & OUT OF BOUNDS EXERCISE

In Bounds	Out of Bounds
_____	_____
_____	_____
_____	_____
_____	_____
_____	_____
_____	_____

Moving forward

One time I was traveling with my family to Disney World. The kids were young, so we had car seats, strollers, snack bags. Plus, all the clothes for the week. We were so loaded down it took us forever to get through security and onto the airplane. It was also awkward and uncomfortable carrying so much baggage.

It was such a relief when we got to the room, and I could put all the bags down.

We all have baggage we carry around with us. If someone offends you, put it in the bag. Someone is rude to you, someone else talks behind your back. Into the bag it goes with everything else.

We can get loaded down with life if we aren't careful.

Take my advice and travel light. That means letting go of the offense. Instead of complaining about it, we need to simply let it go.

Once you let go of the past, you can move forward to your destiny. You can fulfill your dreams because nothing is holding you back or weighing you down.

Here are five reminders to help you move forward:

1. What someone thinks of you does not define you. People's opinions are based on their own perspectives, not your worth. Your value is not determined by the approval or judgment of others, but by who you are in God's eyes.
2. Sometimes the only closure you will receive is knowing you tried your best. Closure often doesn't come from others—it comes from within. Trust that your efforts and integrity are enough. You don't need the validation of others to move forward.
3. Not everything you think about yourself is true. Challenge your negative thoughts and replace them with truths. Take time to identify any lies you've been telling yourself and ask God to show you the truth of who you are in Him.
4. Comparing, dismissing, or minimizing your trauma won't make it go away or hurt any less. Acknowledge your pain and allow yourself to heal at your own pace. You don't need to justify your experience to anyone else, and healing is a personal journey that doesn't follow a specific timeline.
5. Unfaced fears will become your limits. When we avoid facing our fears, we unknowingly allow them to control us. But when we face them, we find freedom and strength. Ask God for courage and trust that He's with you every step of the way.

The power of purpose

When you live life on purpose, you can be focused and intentional. I have noticed that a big tipping point for men is having a purpose. Otherwise, we wander aimlessly through life.

Then, when a man finds his purpose, a light goes on in his eyes. Instead of being passive, he becomes passionate about moving forward.

The first program I did after I was saved was Maximized Manhood. We also become passionate about the things that impact us the most. In 2002, Dr. Paul Osteen launched the program at Lakewood.

Approximately 1,000 men showed up at the launch. Do you know how many graduated? It was either 33 or 34. That one-year program changed me. It taught me how to be like Christ. As I understood my purpose, I stepped out and started to lead. Little did I know I'd be overseeing the program almost 25 years later.

I love when women come up to me at the graduation and tell me they got a new husband. He's the same husband but he's different. He understands his purpose.

I think God has a sense of humor. Women complain about their husbands being passive, but they have no problem leading the household. Why did God make us so passive but at the same time call us to leadership?

I believe the disconnect comes in our lack of purpose in life.

Once we learn who we are in Christ and that we have a new identity, everything changes including us. As our perspective shifts, we shift into our destiny. I see men's lives totally change as they embrace their new identity and connect with their purpose. That's why men become so passionate about seeing other men go through the program too.

Freedom in India

The same thing happened with Pastor Anuradha Das from India. When we launched the Freedom Program during the pandemic, we had no idea that a woman from New Delhi would become one of our greatest advocates.

Pastor Anu was so impacted by ***Your Freedom Journey*** that she has a vision of taking 5,000 pastors there through the program.

India is a shame-based culture. A big part of Freedom is getting the shame out and owning your story. Not only did that happen for her, but now I'm receiving story after story from India of life change. She now has a purpose that is impacting a nation.

Seasons

We all go through seasons in life. Some are more challenging than others. Like the changing of the seasons, we may go through some winter times and then springtime.

When you have the right perspective, you know that what is happening in your life is temporary, and God will use it to produce fruit in your life. In his book Connecting the Dots, Joel Malm shares how every new season starts with a turning point. Something happens that changes things. It could be an unexpected loss, kids go off to college, your parents get a divorce, or you go through a divorce.

The truth is, we will all go through different seasons. The saying, "this too will pass" is true. It is difficult when you are in a hard season, but it is temporary. You can grow through it and become better. God is preparing you for what's ahead.

You are not a mistake. God says you are a masterpiece. Don't let something from your past or present keep you from reaching your full potential. You have a destiny to fulfill. Like Pastor Anu, you can break free from what has held you back.

Now let go of the past and move forward into your purpose. You were made for more!

Chapter Fifteen

FLY FREE

The power of forgiveness

There once was a bird who was meant to fly free. He was born to soar high in the sky.

One day, a man captured the bird and put him in a cage. The bird hated the cage. He also hated the man who had put him in the cage. He would turn away every time the man came into the room and refused to even acknowledge him. Each day the bird got angrier and angrier about being caged. He would stare out the window and watch the other birds flying free. He daydreamed about being free and enjoying life. Stressed out, he started losing his feathers and lost his appetite.

The man didn't understand what was wrong with the bird and left the cage open so the bird could get out. The bird felt like the man should make up for what he had done. He became bitter and refused to leave.

The man took the bird out of the cage to release him, but the bird couldn't enjoy his newfound freedom. His dreams never came to pass. So, the bird flew back into the cage. I'll show him, thought the bird. Eventually, the bird died.

He had lived in a cage of his own making. He was born to fly free but he was limited by the cage in his mind.

Like the bird, many of us live in a cage of our own making because we struggle with forgiving someone who hurt us or moving on past an event where we lost something or someone. We get stuck and can't move forward.

Breaking free

To truly fly free, we must first recognize that forgiveness is not about the other person—it is about setting ourselves free. Here are a few ways to break free from the cage of unforgiveness:

1. **Acknowledge the hurt** – Denying or suppressing pain only prolongs our suffering. Recognize what happened, how it made you feel, and how it has affected your life.
2. **Make a choice to forgive** – Forgiveness is a decision, not just a feeling. You may not feel ready, but choosing to release resentment allows healing to begin.
3. **Let go of expectations** – We often wait for an apology or for the person who hurt us to make amends. But true freedom comes when we release the need for others to fix what they have done.
4. **Shift your focus** – Instead of dwelling on the past, focus on your present and future. Ask yourself: What kind of life do I want to live? How can I move forward with peace and joy?
5. **Seek support** – Healing is not always easy. Whether through friends, counseling, journaling, or prayer, finding a support system can help in the process of letting go.
6. **Embrace your freedom** – Once you choose to forgive, allow yourself to experience life fully again. Like the bird was meant to soar, so are you.

Forgiveness does not mean what happened was okay. It does not mean forgetting. It means choosing peace over bitterness, healing over pain, and freedom over being trapped.

You were born to fly free. Don't let the past keep you caged. Open the door, spread your wings, and embrace the life that is waiting for you.

A cage of our own making

Jesus said,

"If you forgive the sins of any, they are forgiven them; if you retain the sins of any, they are retained."[142]

This is also how issues are passed down from one generation to another. If you don't release them, they cling to you and can be passed down to your children.

Have you ever noticed how some people become like the very thing they hated?

For instance, a boy may hate how his dad would come home drunk every night and would live in fear of his anger. "I'll never be like him", he proclaims. But he becomes just like him. Why? Because he held it against his dad. He didn't forgive him and let it go.

Do you want to get well?

One day, Jesus came to a pool where periodically Angels would stir up the waters and heal people. There was an invalid man who had laid there thirty-eight years. He had lots of excuses about no one helping him into the water.

Jesus asked him something interesting. "Do you want to get well?"

Sometimes we can be so used to our condition, it becomes our identity. If we get healed, then what do we do?

Let me ask you the same question: **Do you want to get well?**

If you do, you'll have to release whatever has held you back and give it to God. Releasing it means letting it go and not picking it back up again.

One of the exercises we do at encounter retreats is to write our sins on a block of wood. We then throw the block of wood into the fire and let it burn. In that way we release it, and it is gone. We can't pick it back up.

---

142. *John 20:23*

Seventy times seven

Peter asked Jesus, how many times do I need to forgive someone who offends me, seven times? Jesus replied seventy times seven. Most people simply say Jesus gave such a high number because it doesn't matter how many times someone does us wrong, we should forgive them every time. It may seem impossible but thankfully Jesus made a way.

Bought at a price[143]

There were two men who worked for a king. One of the servants owed the king millions of dollars. The king was going to throw him in prison, but the servant begged, and the king forgave him the full amount of what he owed.

That servant then went out and found another servant that owed him several hundred dollars. He demanded the servant pay what he owed him. The man begged him, but the servant showed no mercy. He had him thrown in jail until he could repay his debt.

Another servant who saw what happened, went and told the king. The king became angry and had the servant thrown in jail until he could pay back his huge debt.

This is exactly what God did for us through Jesus. Our sins are many. More than we could pay. God redeemed us through Jesus. It's a debt we could never pay on our own.

Paul said, for all have sinned and fall short of the glory of God[144]. Like the servant who owed millions of dollars, we could never be right with God on our own. We needed a savior who would pay our debt for us.

Paul went on to say, "and all are justified freely by his grace through the redemption that came by Christ Jesus"[145]

---

143. Matthew 18:21-35
144. Romans 3:23
145. Romans 3:24

The bottom line
So, when it comes to forgiveness, since God forgave us so much, how could we not forgive someone who does us wrong. Like the servant who owed a little, we need to forgive people who have offended us.

The consequences are great if we don't.

What forgiveness isn't
Forgiveness doesn't say that what they did was ok. What forgiveness does is release you from being tied to it.

When I was a child, there was a boy in school who bullied me. I was small for my age. He would hold me down and try to make me call myself negative things. This stuck with me for years. In fact, it motivated me to work out, but I would still be nervous when he walked in the room. I would daydream about how to get him back or bad things happening to him. He had gone on with his life and probably never had a second thought about what he had done. I have also come to realize that he was probably responding this way because of negative things happening at home or somewhere in his life.

See forgiveness really isn't about the other person. It's about you. You are not saying what they did was ok. You are not saying they shouldn't be judged or experience consequences for what they did. You are simply saying, I am not going to let this person or situation control my life. I am going to release it and let God be my vindicator.

Easier said than done

Dr. Paul Osteen said, "Forgiveness is a process". It may not happen overnight, and you may need to let it go repeatedly.

I'm not saying it is easy. Forgiveness is hard. What's harder? Not forgiving and having the regrets of holding onto the experience for too long. The regret of having it limit you and what you could have achieved. The regret of seeing families and friends divided and holding grudges until their deathbed.

FORGIVENESS IS A KEY TO FREEDOM

It's a matter of life and death

Unforgiveness is bad for your health. Research shows that holding onto wrongdoings can affect your cardiovascular system, your brain, and your immune health — and may contribute to chronic health problems.

Yes, it's been widely researched and proven that unforgiveness increases stress, depression and anxiety, social isolation, and even compromised physical health due to stress on one's immune system.[146]

Have you ever seen someone who is bitter? They walk around angry and ready to lash out at whoever crosses their path. You don't want to be that person. Sadly, they are only really hurting themselves, and their health.

Disagreement homes

We were on vacation in Croatia and walking down the sidewalk along the Adriatic Sea. There were these beautiful homes along the coast but many of them were boarded up and empty. I asked the person walking with me why and he said, these are disagreement houses. Families would get angry with each other and become divided. The houses would end up falling apart because the family members wouldn't or couldn't work things out. So instead, they sat empty.

How many homes have fallen apart because we just couldn't get over an argument or something that happened?

---

146. *Journal of Health Psychology*

What is forgiveness?

Forgiveness tends to fall into two different categories. There is emotional forgiveness and decisional forgiveness

Emotional forgiveness is when you experience an emotional change and feel like forgiving the person who did you wrong.

Decisional forgiveness is where you make a decision to forgive someone even if you don't "feel" like forgiving them. You know it is the right thing to do and so you make the decision to forgive them. It may take some time before your feelings catch up with the decision.

Making forgiveness a lifestyle

Did you know forgiveness could be a lifestyle or way of life? I call it being hard to offend.

Most of us have been hurt. I was deeply betrayed by someone close to me. It took some time, but I forgave them. It started off as a decision to forgive. I know the exact moment years later that I felt whole and had healed from the experience.

Later, the person I forgave went through a challenging time and didn't know where else to go for prayer. I prayed for them without feeling any animosity. I couldn't have done that if I hadn't forgiven them.

But when you can forgive, you open yourself up for better experiences. I have seen miracles come out of negative experiences because someone chose to forgive.

Being hard to offend is when you come to the realization that hurting people hurt people. As long as you are good on the inside, then the problem must be with them.

I don't ever intentionally hurt someone, so if I do - maybe they took something I said the wrong way or assumed I meant something I didn't - I am quick to apologize. Nothing makes people who are unhappy madder than if they can't get to you. I'll say something like, "Are you ok? Can I pray for you?" They want you to be mad too and when you don't sink to their level, they don't know what to do.

The Forgiveness Letter

One of the ways we've developed to help people release themselves is the Forgiveness Letter. Basically, you are writing a letter to whoever offended you. It could even be you.

In this letter, you forgive the person that hurt you and express the way you feel and give it to God to handle.

You don't have to give it to the person. The power of the letter is the act of getting it out. What you are doing is releasing it.

Here's the question: **Do you want to fly free?**

Freedom challenge

Write a forgiveness letter to each of the people who have offended or hurt you. That might include forgiving yourself. While God doesn't need our forgiveness, you might need to write Him a letter of forgiveness too.

Remember, once you write it out, you don't have to give it to the person. You might get rid of it symbolically by tearing it up, crumbling it up or safely burning it.

As you do, release it to God. Let it go. You might even say something like, "God, I release my unforgiveness to you and ask you to take this burden from me. I forgive _____ and release it to you, I thank you for healing my heart and making me whole, in Jesus' name."

Are you ready to fly free? If you will let go of offenses and forgive those who hurt you, I believe and declare you will experience total freedom in Jesus' name.

FORGIVENESS SAMPLE LETTER

- The Forgiveness Letter can be as long or short as you need it to be
- It's about getting the hurt out and giving it to God to heal
- It does not justify what someone did but releases it from your life
- It allows God to redeem your story and turn it into a testimony
- It sets you free from bondage

Dear _____,

What did they do/not do or what happened (Situation)?

You weren't there for me as a child. You were always too busy to spend time with me. We always had to determine what mood you were in and we had to tiptoe around you. You would yell at me frequently and say terrible things.

How did that hurt you (Acknowledge the pain)?

Your words negatively impacted my self-image and the way I think of myself. I struggle with my self-esteem. I also missed out on opportunities to learn skills that would have helped me as an adult. Even when you did things with me you ended up blaming me when things didn't go well. I don't have good memories of our times together.

How has it impacted your life (Result)?

I have gone through life feeling like I couldn't accomplish anything because of your words and actions. My mind is often filled with thoughts about not being good enough. I doubt myself and my worth.

Closing:

I release you now according to John 20:23 that says what we forgive we release and what we don't forgive we retain. You no longer have a hold over me in this area. What you did is not alright, but I give it to God and ask Him to heal my heart. The rest of my life will be the best of my life!

I now say goodbye to the things that you did to me and forgive you for what you did to me. I pray for Jesus to heal you in this area and that he will impact your life in a deep and meaningful way. If you don't know Christ, I pray that you let him into your heart and that you find the salvation that only comes through Jesus Christ.

In Jesus name, _____.

FORGIVENESS LETTER

Date: _____

Dear _____, (Person who hurt you)

In Jesus Name, _____ (Your Signature)

Chapter Sixteen

TAKE THE MASK OFF

Most people go through life hiding something that they've been through, did to someone else or had done to them.

See - just like with forgiveness - what we hold on to we keep but what we let go of we release. Sharing your story is a form of release.

Putting on masks

Masks are for our protection. We are afraid of people seeing us the way we truly are and not accepting us.

If they knew this about me, they wouldn't like me.

Fear of rejection, disconnection, and shame are understandable protection mechanisms. But who are you really?

Can you be yourself with anyone? Do you put different masks on for different groups of people? Are you the same or different at work and home?

My dad was always angry when I was growing up. We would ask each other when we got home what kind of mood dad was in. We had to walk on eggshells.

When you are younger, you can put on masks and act nice around people. If you don't deal with life's issues now, when you get old you don't care about putting the mask on. What was once on the inside now shows up on the outside. If you are ugly on the inside, you will be ugly on the outside.

Your story matters

No one knows your story better than you. It may sound unrealistic to you right now, but someone needs to hear your story. Someone else is going through something similar or can relate to what you've been through.

Hiding your story and what happened to you is shame based and will hold you in bondage. That's what I mean by your story owning you. When you hold it in, it can turn to bitterness. It's true that hurting people hurt people. Don't waste another day hurting and carrying the weight of unforgiveness.

The dash (-)

When we die, there will be two dates on our gravestone. It will show the day we are born and the day we die. Separating the two is a simple dash. That dash represents the time we are alive on earth.

You may have spent your dash being selfish, had a challenging childhood, life may have been unfair. But can I tell you, the rest of your life can be the best of your life.

The good news is that God says He will work everything even those unfair situations together for your good. As you go through putting your life story down on paper, you will start to see patterns. Maybe you will recognize where God protected and sustained you. The same thing that you felt was holding you down may become your purpose. Nothing you've been through is wasted.

Get ready, you are about to be propelled into your destiny.

Now, don't waste your dash. The time we have right now is too precious to not enjoy it.

If Job was here, he would tell you that he went through unfair things. He lost everything. He didn't do anything wrong. He could've been bitter. But God restored him and gave him double for his trouble. His latter days were greater than his former days.

Proverbs 4:18 says, "The path of the righteous is like the morning sun, shining ever brighter till the full light of the day". There are brighter days ahead for you.

There is healing in the revealing

I spend a lot of time helping people with their stories. I've heard amazing stories of how people have been hurt. It is so sad how many people were molested as children. It sets people on a path of pain, and they try to cope with the pain. But no matter how much you try to cover the pain; it doesn't go away until you "get it out".

When you own your story, you say:
- I struggled with drugs and alcohol but now I am getting the help I need to overcome my addiction.
- I was raped and it's not ok, but I have forgiven those who hurt me and I am free to live an amazing life.
- I had an abortion, and I have to live with that but I forgive myself and am moving forward.
- I was abused as a child, and it led to drug addiction and promiscuity, but I am free now and becoming everything God created me to be.
- I was addicted to pornography but now my wife is holding me accountable and I'm dealing with the issues that led me to this struggle.
- I struggled with homosexuality and was afraid people won't accept me if they knew, but now I am open about my struggle and I'm seeking God in my situation.

It's brave to own your story

Brene Brown wrote an amazing book called *Daring Greatly*. In her research, she found in trying to discover how people connect they shared their fear of disconnection. We were made for connection but what drives us is this fear of disconnection so instead we hide in shame.

It all started with Adam and Eve. They were in a relationship with God, naked and unashamed. But when they did the one thing, he asked them not to do, their first response was to hide in shame. Adam also blamed Eve. When we are exposed, we do two things: Hide & Blame

Owning your story is about getting the shame off you so you can get to your rightful position of being open and honest about who you are. There is freedom on the other side of vulnerability.

OWNING YOUR STORY IS A KEY TO FREEDOM

Men don't like to be vulnerable. We would rather stay at home and watch sports. We shrink back and become passive. If you will trust the process of redeeming your story, it will change your life and the life of others.

Owning your story allows you to show up with confidence and be seen as the leader God created you to be. It also gives room for God to redeem your story.

Brene Brown said, "Courage is showing up and allowing yourself to be seen."[147]

Ask yourself: Do you struggle with sharing your story? What makes sharing your story difficult? Are you honest with people about your story? How deep do you go? What is holding you back? Why are you holding back?

Shame off you

We grew up hearing shame on you. You didn't live up to your parents' expectations, shame on you. You got caught in a lie, shame on you. You were late to school, shame on you.

Shame can hold people hostage. We are afraid to be our true selves because we think that people won't like us if they knew the truth about us.

---

147. *Brene Brown, Daring Greatly,* 2012

When Adam and Eve were in the garden, they were deceived into being disobedient to God. When God asked Adam where he was, he responded by hiding and then blaming Eve.

We put on masks and pretend to be who we think people want us to be. People have been hurt by religion because they've been taught that they must act a certain way. We judge people and reinforce this shame-based culture.

The truth is, there is freedom on the other side of being open. Once you get the shame out, you feel lighter. That shame is heavy. Jesus said,

> "Come to me, all you who are weary and burdened, and I will give you rest. Take my yoke upon you and learn from me, for I am gentle and humble in heart, and you will find rest for your souls. For my yoke is easy and my burden is light."[148]

Once you get the shame off you, suddenly you can be yourself.

Do you ever act differently depending on who you are with? You are one way with your friends, another way at work, and another way at church. That sounds exhausting, doesn't it?

Next time someone says, shame on you, you can confidently say, no, shame off me.

> "The more you talk about negative things in your life, the more you call them in. Speak victory not defeat. Why don't you start believing that no matter what you have or haven't done, that your best days are still out in front of you."
>
> Joel Osteen

---

148. Matthew 11:28-30

The power of vulnerability

Shame will tell you: You're the only one going through "that" and no one will accept you if they knew "that" about you.

> "Therefore, there is now no condemnation for those who are in Christ Jesus."
>
> Romans 8:1

You're not alone

We often believe we're the only ones struggling. But the truth is, no temptation or hardship is unique to just one person — someone else has walked a similar path. Your story isn't just for you; someone else needs to hear it to find the courage to open about their own story.

Fear of rejection

"If they knew this about me, they wouldn't accept me." Shame convinces us to hide, keeping us from true intimacy. If you struggle with pornography, you may find it difficult to connect deeply with your spouse—because lust never satisfies. It's a never-ending hunger, filling a void only Jesus can truly fill.

Truth: Authenticity is attractive. When you choose to be real, your relationships become richer and more meaningful.

Wearing masks

When we wear masks, we must keep pretending. But the weight of deception is exhausting, and eventually, the truth catches up with us. We often act like we have it all together—like we're perfect.

Truth: None of us are. When we own our story and take off the mask, we experience true freedom. It feels like a weight lifted off our shoulders.

Redemption

There is freedom on the other side of discomfort. When we bring our shame into the light, God redeems our story—not just for us, but for others.

Your mess is your message. Your test is your testimony. Your trial is your triumph.

Been to prison? There's a prisoner who needs to hear how you made it on the outside. Overcome addiction? Someone still struggling needs to know there's hope.

Do it afraid

You don't have to share your story with everyone but share it with someone. Do it afraid. Healing begins in honesty.

The truth is there is Freedom on the other side of fear. Your story could be the key to someone else's breakthrough.

The more you share it the easier it gets. Be authentic and real. Just be yourself and share from the heart. You'll be glad you did.

Most people are afraid of being vulnerable. It's not easy. Do it afraid. God had to encourage Joshua many times to be strong and courageous. To me sharing is one of the bravest things you can do. Holding it in and suffering and acting out of your hurt and hurting others defines living in bondage.

A friend of mine recently shared how she went to a seminar where the speaker said that thing you are afraid of, that's exactly what you need to do.

Take your fear and kick it in the face. You must face your fears.

Take the mask off

Men are notorious for wearing masks. We weave a web of lies and then spend our time and effort keeping up with them.

I always tell single women to be friends with someone for nine months to a year before getting into a serious relationship. Why? Because a guy is going to tell you what you want to hear. He can only keep up the facade for so long before his lies catch up to him. Most every time someone shortcuts this advice, they regret it.

One time, I had a single mom disappear for about three months. The next time I saw her at church, she introduced me to her new husband. She had been hiding because she knew what I would have said. He ended up having problems with drugs she wasn't aware of and became abusive. He ended up in prison and she had children to raise without a dad.

It's so freeing when you finally take the mask off and be who you really are. To be who God created you to be.

God wants to redeem your story. Nothing you've been through is wasted.

I've already shared that God is working all things together for your good and His glory.

If there is something on the inside that says, "they wouldn't like me if they knew this about me". That's what you need to get out.

The truth is, once you get the shame out the enemy has no hold on you. It's out in the open. When you keep it hidden in shame, the enemy can play with your mind.

Mess into message

The surprising thing is when you share your story you will be amazed by how many people have gone through the exact same thing.

> "God knows how to bring greatness out of a great mess."
> Joel Osteen

The enemy wants you to believe that you are the only one struggling with the lust of pornography, alcohol or that you've been to prison, but once you open up, all of a sudden, your mess becomes your message. Your test becomes your testimony. Your trial, your triumph.

Many times, your ministry is birthed out of your pain. What you thought discredited you will propel you into your destiny.

We all have a story. What's yours?

Here is a process you can use to share and refine your story. The good news is that everyone has a story. That means you have one too. The other good news is that no one knows your story better than you. So, share it from the heart.

David's life story example:

We all have a story! King David had a story. This is all written down for us in 1 and 2 Chronicles and 1 and 2 Samuel. It doesn't get more public than that. The good, the bad and the ugly.

I've used King David's life story as an example:
- He was a shepherd and spent a lot of time hanging out with sheep. Not so exciting. But he learned responsibility
- Samuel anoints him as king, but he goes back to the shepherd's field.

He was the last one his father thought of as a potential king
- Delivers lunch to his brothers and runs into destiny of single-handedly fighting Goliath
- Plays harp for King Saul. Finds favor with the King
- People start singing Saul killed one thousand, David ten thousand. Jealousy sets in and Saul tries to kill David (Throws spear at him)
- Saul pursues David (wilderness years)
- David's men wanted to stone him. The enemy took their wives and children
- And David was greatly distressed, for the people spoke of stoning him, because all the people were bitter in soul, each

for his sons and daughters. But David strengthened himself in the LORD his God."[149]

- They recovered all
- Saul and family killed
- David anointed King over Judah and later King over all of Israel
- David should have been off fighting but stays back and falls in lust with Bathsheba [149]
- Gets Bathsheba pregnant and kills her husband to cover it up
- Nathan rebukes David and he takes feedback to heart
- David's son dies (Consequences for sin)
- Solomon's Born
- David's son Absolom kills his other son Amnon for raping his daughter Tamar
- Bitter Absolom tries to take the kingdom from David (Conspiracy). David flees
- Absolom dies. David mourned
- David makes Solomon King
- David dies

---

149. 1 Samuel 30:6

FREE TO SOAR • 215

DAVID'S LIFE STORY
Example

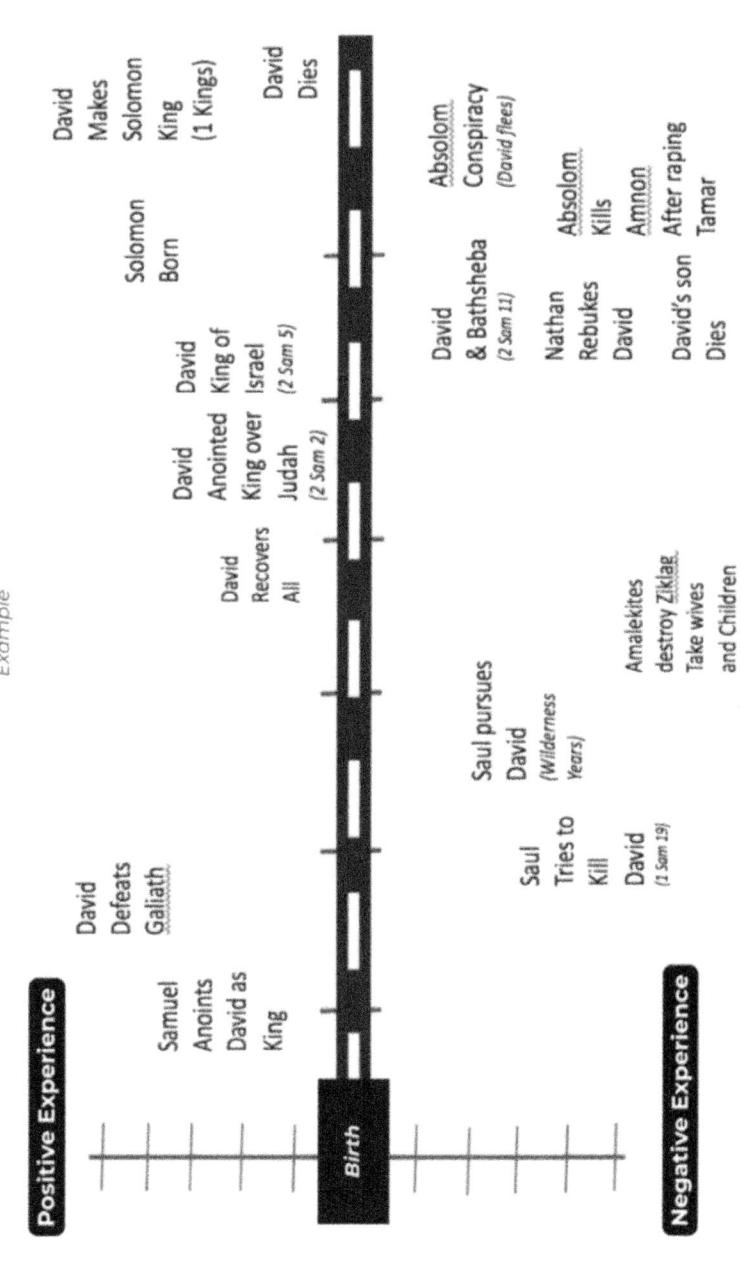

Positive Experience

- Samuel Anoints David as King
- David Defeats Goliath
- David Recovers All
- David Anointed King over Judah (2 Sam 2)
- David King of Israel (2 Sam 5)
- Solomon Born
- David Makes Solomon King (1 Kings)
- David Dies

Birth

Negative Experience

- Saul Tries to Kill David (1 Sam 19)
- Saul pursues David (Wilderness Years)
- Amalekites destroy Ziklag Take wives and Children
- David & Bathsheba (2 Sam 11)
- Nathan Rebukes David
- David's son Dies
- Absolom Kills Amnon
- After raping Tamar
- Absolom Conspiracy (David flees)

LIFE STORY
Birth - Present

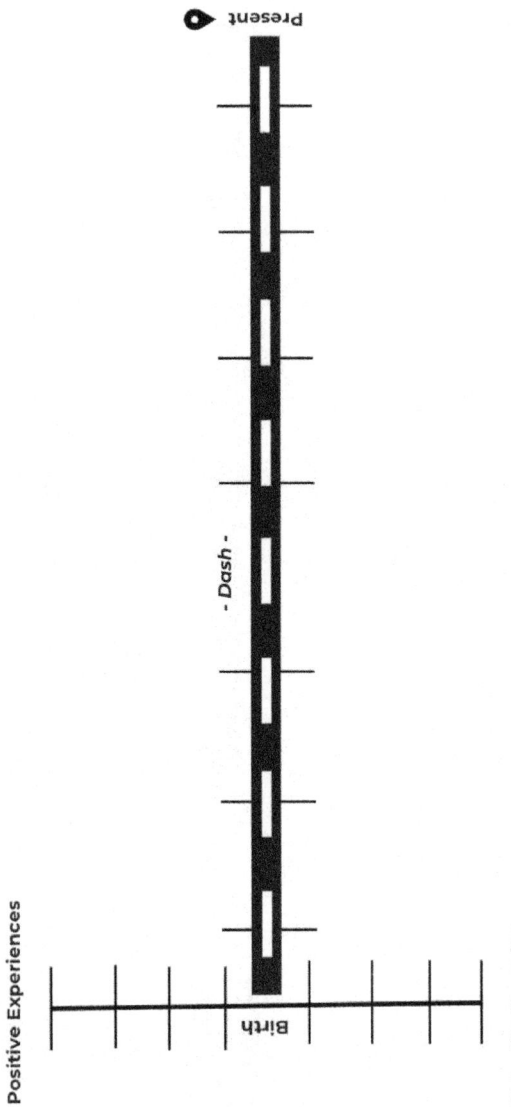

- Dash -

Present

Birth

Positive Experiences

Negative Experiences

Chapter Seventeen

WHAT'S YOUR STORY?

There is power in your testimony!

What's a testimony?
Your testimony is a personal recounting of your salvation experience. It can also be aspects of your life story that impacts and encourages someone through your experience and points them to Jesus. .

Testimonies build other people's faith. You may think you are the only one going through something or that something has happened to you alone, but your message is going to set someone else free. Someone is going through something like what you've experienced.

Life Stories were about you. It was about getting the shame out and allowing God to redeem your story. Testimonies are about helping others by encouraging them that there is hope.

The life story and testimony both serve a purpose
Your testimony points people to Jesus who saved you. It explains why you are willing to help and serve others the way you do.

They can overcome any addiction, depression, hurt, unforgiveness, sickness and become emotionally whole. Your testimony can lift someone up who is down. If God did it for you, He can do it for them!

> "They have conquered him by the blood of the Lamb and by the word of their testimony. And they did not love their lives so as to shy away from death. "
>
> Revelation 12:11

Your testimony should always point people to God. Find a scripture reference that connects to your story.

Within your life story, you will have several testimonies. I have one for salvation, divorce, forgiveness, finances, second chances, going from anxiety to peace, and more being written all the time.

Testimonies open people up and give them permission to share about their own struggles.

As a quick example, I wasn't saved until I was 35 years old. That will speak to someone. It's never too late. I wasn't necessarily a bad guy, but I did things for my own glory, not God's. I had selfish ambitions. Then when I was saved, God started to transform my heart. I started to love people and want to help them with the right motives. It's never too late for God to use you for his glory.

Life stories are messy. Testimonies are more polished. I encourage you to practice your testimony and ask someone you trust for constructive feedback.

I watched as my good friend Ruby went from overcoming the pain of her past, forgiving someone who hurt her and sharing her Life Story with others. Then she was given the opportunity to share her testimony with Middle School children. I watched as hundreds of kids responded to her message and came forward when she encouraged them to forgive whoever has hurt them. It was such a picture of redemption.

> "People don't care how much you know until they know how much you care"
>
> Teddy Roosevelt

It builds trust

Sharing your testimony with others accelerates building trust with others. This is a great icebreaker in connecting with others. Asking someone else to share their story is a great way to show you care.

Active listening, being present, showing empathy and asking questions is an important way to build rapport and build a healthy relationship.

It Gives God Glory

Testimonies help people relate to God. They make Him real and come alive for someone else. He's not some far off God but a Good Father who cares about his children.

Testimonies open people up to salvation. They touch people's hearts and turn your:

Test into Testimony

Vice into Victory

Mess into Message

Wreck into Recording

Trial into Triumph

Forgiveness into Freedom

Graves into Gardens

We all have a story

I was teaching inmates on Owning Your Story at the Bell Prison Unit in Cleveland, Texas. During our small group discussion, one of the inmates kept his head down. He had tattoos all over his body including his face. You could tell he had been beat down by life.

When it was his turn to share, he looked up and said, no one has ever told me I have a story. He shared how he had been abused as a child and like many kids was riding the trains. He lit up a little bit and said I now know I have a story that someone needs to hear.

We all have a story.

A, B, C . . . It's as easy as 1, 2, 3 . . .
The ABCs of sharing a testimony are so valuable:
- **Authentic** – Speak from the heart. People connect with realness, not perfection.
- **Brief** – Get to the point; don't let the details overshadow the message.
- **Clear** – Make it easy to understand; clarity brings impact.
- **Compelling** – Your story should inspire hope, healing, or change.
- **Tailored to Your Audience** – Different people need different parts of your story. Share what will help them most.

Your Story. His Glory

The reason we tie scripture to our stories is to pull God into to help people see how He is in your story.

For instance, one of my testimonies is about feeling anxious when my now ex-wife left me. I went through an unexpected divorce. I was overwhelmed and felt anxious.

Have you ever felt anxious and not known what to do? I lost lots of weight, but I can tell you it's not the best weight loss program. I had to learn to be ok with being alone.

As I mentioned before, that's when I found where it was written and memorized Philippians 4:6-7. It's about not feeling anxious but receiving His peace.

It didn't change over-night, but any time I felt anxious, I spoke those words over my situation. Pretty soon I stopped feeling anxious and started experiencing God's peace. Now any time I even start to feel anxious, I speak that scripture over my life.

Here's some key points about testimonies:
- **Develop long and short versions**. I always have guys timed to a

few minutes to force them to narrow it thoughtfully to the most important parts. Be intentional.
- **Encourage others.** Testimonies encourage others and brings them hope for their situation. They might include: your salvation experience, getting your miracle, overcoming a struggle, the other side of a trial, or how you became financially free.
- **Think about your audience.** It started off about you and healing takes place but eventually it becomes about impacting others. We have enough people who just want to hear themselves talk. *How can your story benefit someone else? Who are you talking to?*

Pastor John Gray is exceptional at this. He makes singles feel like the message is perfect for them and then he can speak at a marriage conference and every married couple relates to what he is saying.

There was a guy at church who just wanted to hear himself talk. Each weekend he would have something he wanted to share, and it didn't matter who he was saying it to. He would go on and on and couldn't read my body language that I wanted to get away.

Your message really doesn't matter if it's not received. Pretty soon I started avoiding him. If I saw him coming, I would go the other direction. You don't want to be that guy.

- **Tailor your message to your audience.** As I said, I can take pieces of my story and share about salvation, forgiveness, redemption, being a single dad, or my financial recovery. What part of your story will be best for your audience?
- **Practice with feedback makes perfect.** Practice your story. Time it. Can you do it in five minutes? Have someone give you feedback about how you can make it even more impactful.
- **Present it.** With your mentor or in a small group, share your testimony with others. This will help you get over the stage fright of a larger group. The guys also need to hear what you have to

say. In fact, people need to hear what you have to say. There is someone right now going through what you overcame who will benefit from your testimony.

Public speaking is a top fear among people. My friend Eileen shared with me two easy techniques to get over stage fright:

1. First say, "I am excited to share". The same feeling of fear can be turned into excitement simply reframing the situation. And,
2. Then say, "They need to hear what I have to say". Encourage yourself because your story matters. Someone out there is going through the same thing right now and needs to hear how you got through it. Now, let's get started on your testimony. Get it down on paper and share it with someone else.

TESTIMONY TEMPLATE

Situation/Before (What was your situation before?):

Process/During (How did things change/What was the process?):

Outcome/After (Where you are now?):

How might you encourage someone else who might be going through something similar?

Scripture Connections (What scripture or scriptures tie best to your testimony?)

What else would you like to share that might be important to your story that you didn't already include?

Chapter Eighteen

NO JUDGMENT ZONE

The longer I live, the less judgmental I have become. Much of that is because of life experiences like going through the struggle of a divorce. Some of it has come through observing others who have been judgmental and seen the consequences of that in their lives. But most of my change has come through Jesus and having him change my perspective.

In our Freedom breakout groups, we don't have a lot of rules. The facilitator is empowered to deal with behavioral issues if they come up. One thing that we do reinforce is to create a "no judgment zone".

What's a no judgment zone?

People, especially in these times, have experienced all kinds of life issues. It is easy to judge people. We've all experienced enough judgment, advice, and people trying to fix us.

Jesus told us to take the plank out of our eyes before we take the speck of sawdust out of someone else's eye. Then we can see clearly to help the other person.

What does it mean to not be judged? What does it mean to be seen, heard, valued, respected and understood?

Or more importantly, what does being seen and not judged look like for you?

I like specific examples. So, let me ask you to share about a time when you felt seen. What happened? What did someone say or do to make you "feel" seen?

A no judgment zone is a place where people can be seen and heard without feeling the judgment of society and sadly religion. A place where they feel safe, accepted and connected.

You want to be free from the torment of your past. The trauma you experienced. The life you thought you'd be living. The disappointments and even the people who let you down.

Have you found that the same people you are or were looking to help you to get free, judged you? Maybe people have done you wrong. It's hard to move forward.

We step over people to get where we want to go but did you actually see them? Do they matter? Or are the road bumps on the journey?

Another question is do they matter to you? Do you see them for who they truly are?

I see you

In Genesis, there's a well-known story of Abraham's wife becoming jealous of her maidservant Hagar. She had pushed Abraham to have sex with her but now was upset about it and wanted her sent away.

Think about Hagar. She didn't ask for her situation. She just wanted to serve and survive. Abraham was old and even though God told them they would have a son, Sarah became impatient.

Have you ever had something unfair happen to you and it wasn't even your fault?

Abraham didn't even argue with Sarah about Hagar's future. He said, "She's your servant, do as you feel is right". So Sarah sent a pregnant woman into the desert. She didn't stand a chance. One of God's names is El Roi, the God who sees.

> She gave this name to the Lord who spoke to her: "You are the God who sees me, "for she said, "I have now seen the One who sees me."
>
> Genesis 16:13

God met Hagar where she was. Out in the middle of nowhere waiting to die. An angel told her that nations would come from her son. She humbled herself and went back to Abraham's camp.

If no one else sees you, God does. You are never alone. You have a destiny to fulfill!

What does it mean to be seen?

One of my favorite movies is Avatar. I can watch it repeatedly. Jake's brother had died, and his DNA matched the Avatar created for his brother. Jake had been disabled in the military and was confined to a wheelchair. He was able to enter the synthetic body of an Avatar and leave the wheelchair. But he had to go to another planet, called Pandora.

At first, he was doing it to win over the Na'vi tribe so the humans could continue to mine the planet. But as he got to know the indigenous and fell in love with Neytiri, his perspective changed. He started to become one of them.

There is a moment when Jake - struggling to breath the Pandora air and no longer in the Avatar body – looks into Neytiri's eyes and says, "I see you". No longer did he see a different species. He saw her for what was inside of her and not the outside. He saw her heart beyond their differences.

This is a great example as well of not judging each other based on the color of our skin.

How do you want to be seen?

I want to be:

- Seen without being judged
- Appreciated
- Valued
- Understood
- Invited without being indicted
- Heard without being fixed
- Loved without conditions

- Cared for without being controlled
- Safe without being isolated
- The real me without the mask
- Confident without being arrogant

Do you see others?

If we are all going to be seen, we must start seeing other people too. When we focus on ourselves and our need to be seen, it is self-focused. If you want to be seen, you must take the first step and start seeing others first.

Do you remember the principle that tells us we will reap what we sow? If you want to be seen, see others. Plant some "being seen" seeds.

The gift of presence

There are so many distractions vying for our attention. It can be challenging to be present and focus on the person you are talking to without judging them and being distracted by our thoughts or other things going on around us.

The Gift of Presence is being present in the moment. It means giving someone your undivided attention and caring enough about them to want to listen, get to know them, be curious about their lives and ask questions.

Have you ever been in a conversation and you're so busy thinking about what you're going to say that you don't hear a word the other person is saying. Or, have you been in a conversation with someone who doesn't seem to care what you have to say, they just want to talk about themselves? I usually just stay quiet in those moments and let them talk. It would be a waste of my time to try to say anything.

There was someone in my life who always thought she was right. It didn't matter what I said, I couldn't convince her that I wasn't thinking what she thought I was thinking or that her view of the situation or circumstances was off. Some people have a made-up mind and you're not going to change it.

Of course, we should make up our minds and be intentional about who we should listen to or spend our time with. Our time is too valuable to waste it with closed-minded people.

That doesn't mean we should be rude. We can always be nice to others and still set boundaries on how much of your time you're going to give to them.

On the other hand, there are people who need you to spend some time with them. People that need your healing words. We all need to be needed. We were made for connection.

As you experience your own healing on your journey to freedom, you will move from doing more of the talking to being able to listen and have healthier relationships with others.

Walk a mile in my shoes

There's an old saying - walk a mile in my shoes - meaning take time to see what it's like to be me before you judge me.

Paul told the Corinthians, "But by the grace of God I am what I am, and his grace to me was not without effect."[150]

I think it is a good perspective to take the position that it's only by the grace of God that you and I aren't in someone else's condition. We don't know what they've been through, what circumstances led up to them being homeless, poor, or even in jail.

I have personally seen parents who judged other parents because of the actions of their children. Then their own children eventually did something worse. When you judge others, you open yourself up. I still maintain a healthy fear of this coming back on me so I would pray for them instead of taking a critical viewpoint.

But by the grace of God my kids turned out the way they did. You just never know. You can have plenty of money, provide all their needs, put

---

150. 1 Corinthians 15:10

them in private school, and they could still end up on drugs and dropping out of school.

Paul also said,

> "My conscience is clear, but that does not vindicate me.
> It is the Lord who judges me."
>
> 1 Corinthians 4:4

What does it mean to have a clear conscience?

When we feel guilty, anxious about life, and have unforgiveness in our hearts, it is difficult to feel content.

When we allow these things to take root, we can be bitter.

In Jewish culture, a bitter plant was a poisonous one. When we hold onto resentment, disappointment, unmet expectations, or hurt feelings, it can take root and poison us spiritually, mentally and physically.

Hebrews 12:15 says,

"See to it that no one falls short of the grace of God and that no bitter root grows up to cause trouble and defile many."

We can also poison ourselves when we are unfaithful to God and go after what the Bible calls idols. Idols are images or representations of a god other than the one true God. It can be anything that we place as more important than God.

When the ruler asked Jesus what he needed to do to inherit the Kingdom of God, Jesus told him to give away all he had to the poor and follow him[151]. This made the man sad because he was very rich. I think we can all relate to his reluctance. It wasn't that God wants us to be poor. But he knows our heart and He wants us to be free.

You may have to give up something that you see as important right

---

151. Matthew 19:21

now but understand that God desires to bring you so much more. More satisfaction. More joy. More abundance. More favor. More life. God is a God of more.

We can put things like money, fame, power, and even people above God. The Israelites were constantly worshiping other gods and were influenced by neighboring tribes.

God had told them not to have relationships with the wrong people because it would influence them to worship other nations' gods. As wise as Solomon was, this was his downfall.

Have you seen in your own life how the wrong influences can impact you and send you in the wrong direction?

When I was a teenager, I met a young guy who was fun to be around, carefree and living outside my norm. It seemed exciting at the time. I tried things I hadn't tried before and did things I wouldn't have done otherwise.

I was rebellious to my parents and thought about running away. I even thought about suicide - something I had never entertained before.

My mom later told me that she knew she had loved me so much when I was little that I would eventually return to them. When he was out of my life things improved and I got back on course.

The Bible says to raise a child in the way they should go, and they will not depart from it.

What if you didn't come from an encouraging family, experience childhood trauma in your childhood?

You can either become like what you experienced or set a new direction for you and your family.

My dad was an angry man. He sat around watching sports on television all day long while I wanted and even asked for him to come throw the ball with me outside. He had a knee injury from when he was young that caused him a lot of pain. I didn't understand that when I was a kid, and he gave me no explanation.

Later he got knee replacement surgery, and he was a different person.

I wish he wouldn't have waited so long but pain can change the way we act toward others.

I could have become bitter. But I wanted to be better.

When I had kids, I made it a point to spend time with them. I'd throw the football with my son and kick the soccer ball with my daughter. I even coached her soccer team, even though I had never played soccer, while she picked flowers on the sideline.

There is still residue from my childhood.

We lived on a golf course and my dad played golf frequently. My brother and I would go with him. I think he brought me along to have someone to blame his bad golf shots on. I can play golf fine, but I don't want to. He took the fun out of the game. I have forgiven him, but I still don't enjoy playing golf.

What has life and life's circumstances taken the fun out of in your life? What would you like God to redeem?

The good news is, He can do it!

I may not want to play golf, but I am not hurt, angry or bitter about it. There are plenty of things I'd rather be doing.

Jesus came to set us totally free

Paul told the Romans,

"Therefore, since we have been justified through faith, we have peace with God through our Lord Jesus Christ, through whom we have gained access by faith into this grace in which we now stand. And we boast in the hope of the glory of God."[152]

Because of what Jesus did for us, Paul continues with another "therefore".

"Therefore, there is now no condemnation for those who are in Christ

---

152. Romans 5:1-2

Jesus, because through Christ Jesus the law of the Spirit who gives life has set you free from the law of sin and death."[153]

The cover up

Are we free to do anything?

Peter said to live as free people, but do not use your freedom as a cover-up for evil; live as God's slaves.[154]

See, we were once slaves to sin because of what Adam did (Original sin). Then because of what Jesus did, we have been set free from sin, but we still can make choices that have consequences, good and bad.

Paul put it this way to the Corinthians, "I have the right to do anything, you say—but not everything is beneficial. I have the right to do anything – but not everything is constructive."[155]

I always like to ask myself, "Is this decision going to bring me closer to or farther from God?"

Occasionally, I will give up coffee for a few weeks. It's challenging because of the caffeine headaches but the reason I do it is to break its control over my flesh. I don't want it or anything other than God to have control over me.

People sometimes don't think about the consequences of their actions. Fortunately, I tend to think about what would happen down the road. One of my strengths is futuristic. I am always thinking ahead.

For instance, if you have an affair, most likely it will lead to divorce. Solomon even said it could lead to death. Can you see it? Try to think about the consequences before you act.

---

153. Romans 8:1-2
154. 1 Peter 2:16
155. 1 Corinthians 10:23; 6:12

The two dogs

Maybe you've heard the story about the two dogs. In one version, an old man shares with his grandson that we all have two dogs inside of us. One is selfish and the other is our spirit. The two are at odds with each other. The grandson ponders this information for a minute and then asks, "which one wins"? The grandfather replies, "The one you feed".

We have free will. We can choose to feed our flesh or feed our spirit, but not at the same time. We can be led by our spirit or led by our flesh. The flesh is our human desires. They tend to lean more selfish and self-serving. Lust is a desire of the flesh. The spirit aligns itself with God's will and tends to lean towards unconditional love and generosity. The two oppose each other.

As you lean into one more than the other, just like when we don't eat, we get weaker. The one you don't feed will fade away.

The good news is, when you give your life to God, you receive the Holy Spirit. You no longer have any obligation to follow your sinful nature.

That's why Paul told the Galatians, "So I say, walk by the Spirit, and you will not gratify the desires of the flesh."[156]

N.T. Wright said,

> "The Apostle Paul gives us markers, signs that we are the new creations pointing the way to a new kind of kingdom. We have put off the ways that marked out our belonging to the old way of life and have been renewed."

---

156. Galatians 5:16

Do it for them

Even though our conscience is clear, God wants us to think about other people's faith. Even though I may regard my own behavior as acceptable to God, He still wants me to think about its effect on others and their faith.

In Jesus' day, there was a lot of concern about eating food that had been sacrificed to false gods. The disciples, and many other initial believers, were Jewish and followed the customs and Law of Moses. They viewed the behavior as sinful and the food as unclean.

As Gentile or non-Jewish believers came in, some people were forcing them to follow the Law of Moses. There were also arguments over circumcision.

Paul managed to solve the food issue by declaring God created everything, therefore nothing dedicated to Him was to be considered unclean. That's why we pray before each meal today. Whatever we eat should first be dedicated to the Lord.

He told the Corinthians, so then, about eating food sacrificed to idols: We know that "An idol is nothing at all in the world" and that "There is no God but one."[157]

Paul shared how what we eat, or drink may not be an issue for us, but someone else may have an issue with it. If you find that to be the case with a friend or family member, don't eat it. Not for the sake of your conscience, but theirs. If the other person doubts that they should partake of anything, they are condemned, because they aren't accepting the food by faith. Paul said, anything not done in faith is sin.[158]

Keep the peace

One person thinks one day is holy, and another every day. Some people worry about food and another person worries about something else. It's not worth arguing about. We all think we are right.

---

157. *1 Corinthians 8:4*
158. *Romans 14:23*

Paul shared how things like food and what we eat, and drink aren't worth arguing about. It's better to keep the peace. He says don't cause someone else to stumble and fall just because you are alright with it.

Let's make the main thing the main thing.

What's the main thing? Jesus. Let's focus on what unites us and not what divides us.

It's great to have a clear conscience but as we are transformed, we won't feel the need to be right all the time, and we will esteem others above ourselves.

We will want to keep the peace, fight for unity, and edify or build others up.

Paul told the Corinthians, "Even though I am free and belong to no one, I have made myself slave to everyone to win as many as possible."[159] He accepted people right where they are. He adapted. He adjusted. He sought to understand people's beliefs. He was a true disciple for Jesus.

He said, "I have become all things to all people so that by all possible means I might save some. I do all this for the sake of the gospel, that I may share in its blessings."[160]

How are your motives?

- Are you doing things to help fill something in yourself or to really care about others?
- Is it hard for you to be alone?

These are important questions as we seek healthy relationships.

---

159. 1 Corinthians 9:19
160. 1 Corinthians 9:22-23

Chapter Nineteen

BIRDS OF A FEATHER

The power of connection

Have you ever heard the saying, "Birds of a feather flock together"? It basically means that people with similar characteristics or interests usually hang out together.

If you want to soar with eagles, you can't hang around turkeys. You show me who you are hanging out with, and I'll show you where you'll be in five years.

The people you hang around with can bring you up or pull you down in life. They can encourage you to be better or hold you down.

> "You can't soar with the eagles as long as you hang out with the turkeys."
>
> Joel Osteen

I was doing prison ministry when I heard a guard tell an inmate, I'll see you back here soon. There is a high recidivism rate which creates a revolving door. The problem is complex, but part of the issue is that many of the inmates go back to their old environment and hang out with their old friends. You may have the best intentions in the world and plan this time to be totally different. The challenge is the temptation, and old patterns kick in and it's difficult to resist. The best defense is a good offense. That means be proactive and change your environment.

You may have to change your friends and who you are hanging around with. Hang around people who build you up and make you better.

Crabs in a bucket

Imagine a bucket filled with crabs. Each crab, yearning for freedom tries to climb out of the bucket. However, what happens next is rather perplexing. Instead of collaborating and assisting each other, the crabs engage in a self-destructive cycle. As soon as one crab manages to reach the edge and is on the verge of freedom, its fellow crabs pull it back down, preventing its escape.

Astonishingly, the collective behavior of the crabs ensures that none of them succeed in breaking free. A form of learned helplessness sets in.

Like the crabs, sometimes we can hold people we love back because of fear. Who do you think you are? Maybe it's because of jealousy, protection or the way we were raised.

The truth is, if your kids better themselves, the whole family rises higher. We can be the catalyst that propels ourselves, our children and our family to new heights.

People may tell you, don't rock the boat, don't make waves, follow the crowd, follow the beaten path. The truth is, God wants you to grow, to go higher, to take a new path. Don't be limited by others.

CONNECTION IS A KEY TO FREEDOM

During my research of what was making a difference in people's lives as they sought to overcome different struggles including addiction, I came across a TED talk where Johann Hari makes the statement that,

"The opposite of addiction is not sobriety; the opposite of addiction is connection."

A common experience for most addicts is this feeling of isolation and an inability to connect in a meaningful way with others and the world around them.

Isolation can also be an attempt at control. It's a way of protecting yourself. I can't control what's going on around me, but I can control this. They may plan on re-connecting at some point once they get it all together. The challenge with isolation is it has the opposite effect. We were made for connection. Isolation works against you.

Your thoughts will tell you that you're better off alone when, in reality, you need people. You need connection. You were made for community.

One another

Over 30 times in scripture, we can read the phrase "one another." Here are a few of my favorites:
- Love one another
- Encourage one another
- Serve one another
- Comfort one another

You need "one anothers" around you.

Laura's story

Right before I met my wife, she went through a period of isolation and disconnection. She had gone through a brief marriage and after two months barely escaped with her life. She struggles with depression and found herself over a period of time pulling away and hiding out.

She came to a Lakewood service to see Bishop T.D. Jakes. He said five words that changed her life path, "Get out of your tent". Those few words really impacted her. She decided right then to find a bible study. A good friend of hers was coming to a bible study at my house once a month and suggested she come. I'm so glad she did.

Laura got out of her tent and connected in community. It changed her life and the rest is His Story.

Tenderloin District, San Francisco

For many years, I took teams to the Tenderloin District of San Francisco where thousands of homeless are confined to this area. There is an amazing ministry there called City Impact who is making a difference.

I liked taking people there because it was different from a normal mission trip. Usually when you travel to other countries, people are open to the gospel and the hope that comes through Jesus. But these homeless people had heard it all before. They have lost hope. They've burned all their bridges and isolated themselves. Sadly, every morning when I walked to a nearby coffee shop, I would pass at least one homeless person who had died during the night. I'd see a needle in their arm or lying next to them.

When we would go out in the streets to pray for them at night, we'd ask them what they'd like us to pray for. I was surprised as most of them wouldn't ask for anything for themselves but to pray for their families. Some of them would ask that they be reconciled with their families.

The challenge to connect

Why do some people have trouble with connection? There are many answers to this question, but through many conversations and asking people to tell me their stories, I have learned that childhood trauma and not being protected by someone they should have been able to trust is a common theme.

There are also behavioral and mental health issues and disorders that can play into this lack of connection for some people. Determining the root cause of someone's struggle with connection may be uncovered through your life story and getting the shame out or it may need to be evaluated by a mental health professional. There is no shame in seeking help.

Be real

In her research, Brene Brown[161] asked people about connection. The interesting thing is they would share examples of their fear of disconnection.

We were made for connection but what drives us is this fear of disconnection so instead of being our authentic selves, we hide in shame and pretend to be someone we aren't.

It all started with Adam and Eve. They were in a relationship with God, naked and unashamed. But when they did the one thing, he asked them not to do, their first response was to hide in shame. When God put Adam on the spot, he blamed Eve.

When we are exposed, we do two things: Hide in shame and blame others. It can be challenging to expose ourselves and be vulnerable. But can I tell you, that's what it takes to have intimacy with someone else.

Brene said we need to show up and let ourselves be seen. That's what being brave looks like. If you want to have healthy relationships, you need to show up and be real.

Toxic relationships

We all desire healthy relationships. The problem is, we are not perfect and can approach life from our own hurts and selfishness. When two people come together it can be challenging to navigate. Over time, cracks start to show.

When I was over the singles ministry, I would always tell the singles. It's not two halves that make a whole but two wholes. I'd encourage them to focus on getting themselves healthy first and then get together with someone else who is healthy.

I would tell the women not to rush in. Give it a year. Men will tell you what you want to hear but eventually their lies will catch up to them.

---

161. Brene Brown, Daring Greatly, 2012

If you are always giving and never receiving, that is an unhealthy relationship.

When we rely too much on other people to meet our emotional needs, we might experience what is called co-dependency. When we have poor boundaries, low self-esteem or difficulty making decisions, others can take advantage of us. We can end up in a dysfunctional relationship.

Control can also be a sign of an unhealthy relationship. When you feel the need to control someone else's behavior or they try to control you, you need to realize that something is off. Many times, abusive partners will use control to keep you in the relationship. They may try to isolate you from your friends and family. They might use what is called gaslighting.

Gaslighting

Many of us have experienced some form of gaslighting in one way or another. It's a way of manipulating people that selfish people use to get what they want from others. They can make us feel we are wrong about how we are seeing the world.

Here's some examples:
- Denial. "That never happened"
- Withholding. "I don't know what you're talking about"
- Deflection. "What about the time you did _____?"
- Shifting Blame. "It is all your fault"
- Countering. "You never remember things correctly"
- Loving words as weapons. "I would never hurt you on purpose"
- Minimizing. "You are overreacting"
- Discrediting. "Everyone thinks you are crazy"
- Rewriting History. "You yelled at me for no reason"

Red flags

I talked earlier in this book about the white flag of surrender, but what about the red flag of run?

How many times have we ignored the red flags of people's behaviors because we want to believe in them or to help them? We want or need their attention. We want to be loved.

When Joseph was a slave in Egypt, he was a faithful servant to Potiphar. You can be faithful, doing all the right things and negative things can still happen to you. People talking about you, trying to manipulate you, coming against you.

One day Potiphar's wife tried to seduce Joseph. What did Joseph do? He ran. The wife caught in her infidelity claimed he raped her. He ended up spending years in prison for something he didn't do.

I heard a sermon one time by Pastor Tommy Barnett called what if Joseph and Samson switched places? That stuck with me. Your character is everything. It is better to run than to compromise.

Those red flags as a Christian are God's warnings that we need to run. Don't ignore the warning signs. There are always consequences, good or bad for our decisions. And relationships are a big decision!

It's not two halves that make a whole

So how do you heal from toxic relationships? It may be difficult at first, but you are already on the right track by working on your identity, self-esteem, owning your story, and being transformed.

You may need to get help from a professional counselor or life coach. You'll have to learn to set boundaries and continue to build your self-esteem.

My wife Laura and I have both experienced unhealthy relationships. We now know what it is like to be in a healthy relationship. One big difference for me is that we accept each other the way we are. Neither one of us is perfect. I love Laura's imperfections. I don't try to change her. I focus on what I love about her and encourage her to be the best version of herself.

When we nag at people and push them to change, it is ineffective. It doesn't work. Shift your focus and see how things might change for the better.

Circle of trust

In the movie, Meet the Fockers, Jack (the dad) shares how Greg (his son in law) is out of the circle of trust. It's a funny example of who we can trust and who we can't. Jack left a note on Greg showing the circle of trust with a dot outside the circle that said Greg next to it. He was outside the circle of trust.

Who's in your circle of trust?

Jesus had an inner circle. He had his core that included Peter, James and John. Then he had his twelve. Then there was his extended group of followers.

Who can you trust? Who can you share some time with, share your innermost feelings, and know they won't share it with someone else?

Who's in your circle of trust?

I'm being serious, take a moment and think about someone who you can trust to be the authentic you with. Who is that person?

Don't worry. If you can't think of anyone, God is going to send someone your way.

Freedom challenge

Evaluate your relationships. Who's in your circle of trust? Are you hanging out with the right people?

It is not easy, but you may need to make some changes. If you will let go of the wrong people, God will bring the right ones into your life. God already has the right people lined up for you.

Inner circle: People who know you, respect you, support you and protect you in a healthy way. This will usually only be one person or a few people. It can be family members, a spouse, best friend, or trusted people.

Positive influences: People who are in your small groups, volunteer ministry, church members and positive people who provide healthy connections for you to thrive.

Acquaintances: People you know or see frequently but you don't have a close intimate relationship with. You have healthy relationships and boundaries, but they aren't friends or family or someone you know well.

Out of circle: People who don't bring out the best in you. Maybe they are a negative influence, a toxic or unhealthy relationship, or they hang around the wrong influences or environment.

Divine connections

Pray right now for God to bring the right people into your life and weed out the wrong people.

As you let go of the wrong people, God will bring you the right people who will encourage you, lift you up and help you move toward your destiny.

Resist the desire to disconnect and isolate yourself. It will have the opposite effect of what you desire. You may think you are protecting yourself, but you will cause yourself more pain. Push yourself to get out of your tent.

As you connect with the right people, you will start to feel a sense of belonging.

CIRCLE OF TRUST
Connection is a Key to Freedom!

Who's in your circle?

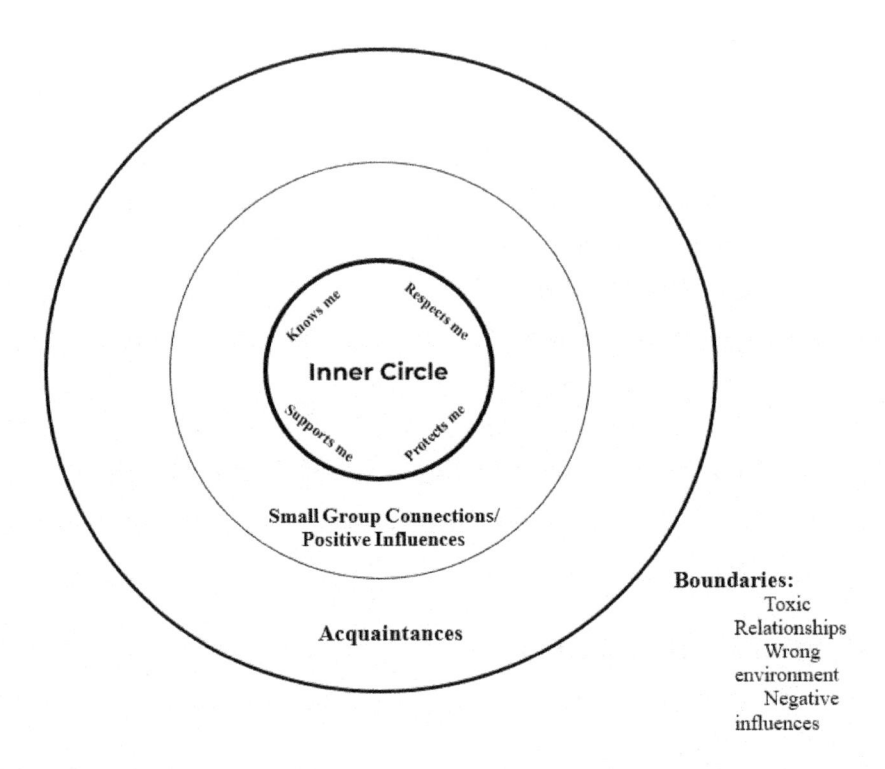

Inner Circle
- Knows me
- Respects me
- Supports me
- Protects me

Small Group Connections/Positive Influences

Acquaintances

Boundaries:
Toxic Relationships
Wrong environment
Negative influences

Chapter Twenty

LIVING LIFE ON MISSION

I have decided to live life on a mission. What's that mean? I don't need to go on a mission trip to a foreign country to help others.

I am on the lookout every day for who God wants me to help that day. It may be a neighbor; it may be a friend. It might even be a stranger or even an enemy.

The key is that I am open and willing to serve God in any capacity. My question for you is, are you willing to serve God no matter the circumstances or inconvenience?

SERVING OTHERS IS A KEY TO FREEDOM

When we serve others, we take the focus off ourselves and our problems. When you help someone in need, all of a sudden, your problems seem smaller.

You've probably heard the saying,

Have a need, sow a seed

I mentioned earlier that you will reap what you sow. It's a Kingdom principle. As I coach others, I usually will encourage them to sow a seed in the area of their struggle.

For instance, if you are struggling with your finances, bring food to an elderly neighbor or help someone who can't pay you back. If you are struggling in your marriage, minister to another couple going through a tough time.

There is always someone who has it worse than you. Instead of having a pity party and asking when someone is going to help me, take the initiative and go help someone else.

There is something powerful that happens when you help someone else. What are the benefits of serving others?

- Gets the focus off your issues
- Re-energizes you
- Include your family and leave a legacy
- Heavenly rewards
- You are blessed to be a blessing
- Sows good seeds

The Good Samaritan

Most of us know the story of the good Samaritan. It is in response to the question, "who is your neighbor?"

In Luke 10, Jesus shares a story to answer the question. There was a man walking down the road. Robbers beat him and took all his stuff. They left him for dead.

A priest and a Levite both walked by and didn't help him. In fact, they crossed to the other side. A Samaritan man was walking along the same road, saw the man and helped him. He not only bandaged him up, he took him to a hotel and paid for his stay.

Jesus then asked, "which one of these was his neighbor? The one who took mercy on the man. We need to go and do likewise."[162]

Living life on mission means being aware of the people around us and responding when needed. Not ignoring or walking past people in crisis.

---

162. *Luke 10:25:37*

Mission minded

My wife is a special woman inside and out. She has an amazing heart for people and a pure spirit. She always gets to know people others would ignore or overlook. I'm so thankful for her!

You don't have to go on a mission trip or even to another country to live life on a mission.

> "Take advantage of every opportunity to be a blessing to others, especially to our brothers and sisters in the family of faith."
>
> Galatians 6:10

Even on vacation, my wife Laura takes time to meet and hear the stories of the local people. Reymundo, for instance, was selling jewelry along the beach. He had sciatica and was in constant pain. She prayed for him to be healed. Later, when she went to see him, one of the other men asked for prayer for his diabetes because Reymundo had been healed.

The day before she had met Carlos who shared how his wife prayed for him every morning before he left the house. He called his wife and let Laura pray with her. The last 8 months had been hard on them because of the impact the pandemic had on tourism in Cancun. Of course, my wife helped them by purchasing jewelry.

I learned how staying at an all-inclusive resort doesn't mean the staff is paid well. When they say "gratuity included" they distribute the money to everyone, and the pay is limited. They still rely on our tips.

We had an incredible waiter named Abraham who had come from Cuba with his family to find a better life. He has two children and is working long hours to provide for his family. He served us the night before and again the next morning. We gladly tipped him.

Here's the "I see you" challenge
Find someone today who you wouldn't normally talk to and ask them their story.

Let them know they are seen.

It might also mean digging a little deeper to find out what someone is going through.

I tried to help a young man for many years, but he couldn't seem to get unstuck. He struggles with rejection because he was taken from his parents in his early teens. When people don't respond to him the right way, he takes it personally and goes to the extreme of blocking them on social media.

Like this young man, you may feel stuck. If you are personally dealing with the same issues repeatedly, ask yourself why. Start paying attention to why you do what you do? There is usually a root cause.

Ask yourself why you respond the way you do? Get to know why someone else does things the way they do. Be curious.

What's my cause?
Many times, your cause is tied to what you've been through. In Freedom, many of our leaders and volunteers have overcome depression, anger, anxiety or addiction. Some have been to prison. Others are veterans or survivors of domestic abuse dealing with post-traumatic stress.

They can empathize with others because of their own personal experiences.

After my divorce, I got a taste of what single moms go through. It's not easy. It created a passion in me to protect and assist single moms and their children.

Nate's story

I have always tended to run to people in crisis. One Sunday at church, a volunteer introduced me to Nate. He was homeless at a bus stop, and she invited him to church. That started a now decade-long friendship and journey toward freedom.

At first, Nate would get angry or offended by someone and I wouldn't see him for weeks. He would shyly show up on a Sunday. When I finally saw him, I would run up and give him a hug. We would go to Starbucks and talk. He expected me to be mad, but I just loved him.

Over time, his running off became shorter and shorter. Because of a childhood trauma, he struggled with sitting in a small group of men. He would frequently get up and go outside to smoke. I told the leaders to let him go and not to make a big deal out of it.

He made it through Anger Management. Funny side story: He started dating and later married Courtney. He was taking her to work and waiting to turn into the parking lot when I saw them. I sped up quickly and honked my horn to scare them. Without realizing who I was, he flipped me off. He felt horrible. I joked with him that I needed his Anger Management certificate back.

Over time he was able to sit in small groups and graduated from Maximized Manhood.

Some of the men at the church helped me rebuild his childhood home that was damaged by Hurricane Harvey. It needed to be gutted. These men gave up every Saturday for a year to serve Nate. He was no longer homeless.

Laura and I are now godparents to Nate and Courtney's two boys. He is still a work in progress, but many people gave up on Nate. This is where we must hold people loosely. Let people be messy and give them room to not be perfect. I want Nate to change but I'm his friend no matter what.

Joel Osteen says, "Give us a year of your life and it will never be the same for the better". One day Nate joked with me, tell Pastor Joel for me that for some of us it's "Give us five years".

We all grow at different rates. Don't compare yourself with others. Life change takes time.

One of my favorite sayings is, "I can't help everyone, but I can help someone". That's very empowering to me. It's easy to feel overwhelmed and not do anything.

What I've learned is to focus on who I can help and not who I can't. Who's in your reach? Who's in your area of influence? Instead of just walking by, stop and engage with them.

The neighbor

My next-door neighbor was a good friend. I was so sad to find out his wife was leaving him for another man. He tried to hold on to the house but after months of trying, he ended up giving it to his ex-wife.

He had let his yard go and the grass was high. I was mowing my yard when I felt God impressing on my heart, you'd mow his yard for him, but would you mow it for her?

So when I reached the end of my yard, instead of turning around I kept on going. I didn't want anyone to see me do it but their daughter saw me. She was very thankful. The next day when they were moving in, I offered to help them move in. Did I like or agree with what had happened? No. But, I felt better, and it opened up a door for a positive relationship without any bitterness or unforgiveness.

What would Jesus do (WWJD)?

It's still a good question today. What would Jesus do? I believe he would:
- Help the least of these
- He would go after the one
- He would forgive and help his enemy
- He would go the extra mile to help someone in need
- He would give self sacrificially for someone else

Pay it forward

I was highly inspired by the movie *Pay It Forward* when it came out at the end of 2000. I was saved one year later. The social study assignment was to put a plan into action that will make the world better.

In the movie, Trevor's project was "pay it forward". He did something nice for someone else but instead of being repaid, he challenged the person to "pay it forward" and do something nice for someone else and so on.

A reporter investigated all these stories of people doing acts of kindness for others and traced them back to one person, Trevor.

That one person could be you!

What if we would all "pay it forward"? What can you do to make the world a better place? Start by helping someone who can't pay you back. Then ask them to pay it forward.

Here are some Serving Other suggestions to get you started:

- Do something simple to bless someone today who can't pay you back
- Do you have an elderly neighbor? Bring them a meal or ask them if they need any help
- Call or text someone you haven't seen or talked to in a while. Let them know you were thinking of them
- See a neighbor whose house isn't mowed? Take a few minutes and mow it for them
- Volunteer for a local shelter or food pantry
- Do you have an expertise? If you're an accountant, help someone in financial trouble
- Invite a friend or coworker to come to service with you this Sunday or join you for Freedom Night
- Do some Spring cleaning and give your unused items to charity

When is someone going to help?
Every once in a while, someone will reach out to me asking when is the church going to help or why isn't the church helping? The better question is what can you do to help or how can I help them? We all function as the hands and feet of Jesus.

If God brought someone across your path and you feel it in your heart, don't get frustrated if others don't respond the way you'd like them to. You can't always pass the buck to someone else. Sometimes the buck stops with you.

What's in your hand?
Do you ever feel inadequate? If you said "yes" then you're in good company. God loves to use people who don't feel like they are good enough, capable enough, or skilled enough.

He doesn't care what side of the tracks you come from, what family you come from, your race, gender or economic status. He only cares if you are available.

We can read in the Book of Exodus that Moses stuttered, was a murderer and didn't feel worthy enough to save God's people from slavery. Moses said to God the old "what if". What if they don't believe me? Have you ever made excuses? What if they don't get healed?

God said to Moses, "What's in your hand?" He had a walking stick. God told him to throw it on the ground to get the attention he was seeking. He ended up using the same rod to part the red sea and deliver his people. God equipped Moses from the start.

Goliath said about David, why did you send this small child. "Am I a dog?" David had a slingshot and five stones, and he defeated a giant.[163]

When Jesus was preaching and the people were hungry, God used a little boy's lunch to feed thousands. Jesus asked the disciples to look around

---

163. *1 Samuel 17:43*

for food. They only found a small boy who brought some fish and bread. Jesus took it and gave thanks. As he broke the pieces they kept multiplying and not only did they feed everyone, but they had leftovers too.[164]

What's in your hand? Maybe it's a hammer to go help repair a home. Maybe you're a nurse who can volunteer some time at a shelter. Or a teacher who can mentor kids after school.

My wife Laura recently went to Guatemala. The team went to help children who had been through trauma. As a teacher who spoke Spanish, it was the perfect opportunity for her to use what skills she has to help others in need. She developed a skit and was able to pray and encourage the young girls.

You may not feel capable or confident enough to step out to help. Can I encourage you that you can make a difference?

Start with helping that one person who's on your heart. Maybe they live next door or around the corner. Maybe you see them at the workplace or where you frequently go to lunch.

You may not feel like you can help everyone but start with helping just one.

---

164. Matthew 14:13-21

Chapter Twenty-One

THE SNIFF TEST

My wife loves watermelons. I am good at picking out the perfect one. We all have our own technique for picking the right fruit. And there is nothing worse than picking the wrong one.

I walk up to the bin full of watermelons at the grocery store and right away I am drawn to one. It has a white spot where it sat in the field while it ripened. Then I thump it with my middle or index finger, and I hear a hollow sound. I may also thump another one to listen to the difference and sometimes select a different one that I think is ready. Nine times out of ten I'm right and the fruit is perfect. Occasionally, I am disappointed as it's over or under ripe.

Jesus said you will know them by their fruit.

The purpose of transformation is for you to bear good fruit. As you are transformed into the image of Jesus, you start to resemble Him in your actions and your deeds.

God's purpose

Earlier, I talked about Romans 8:28 and the fact that we know in all things God works for the good of those who love him.

Now let's focus on the next part that says, who have been called according to his purpose.

So, what is God's purpose for your life? The scripture continues with the answer.

"For those God foreknew he also predestined to be conformed to the image of his Son, that He might be the firstborn among many brothers and sisters."[165]

His main goal for your life is to see you become more like Jesus. To be conformed to His image. To be conformed means to be shaped, molded, or adjusted to fit a particular pattern, standard, or set of expectations - often without questioning it. God wants us to be molded into the form of Jesus.

An inside job

Jesus said, "For no good tree bears bad fruit, nor again does a bad tree bear good fruit, for each tree is known by its own fruit. For figs are not gathered from thornbushes, nor are grapes picked from a bramble bush. The good person out of the good treasure of his heart produces good, and the evil person out of his evil treasure produces evil, for out of the abundance of the heart his mouth speaks."[166]

What's on the inside of a person will be manifested on the outside. We've been working on the Lead Indicators so that you can produce the fruit of life change from the inside out.

We've been working on changing from the inside out. As we become "whole" and complete on the inside, our behavior or what people see are your pure motives. You react with character.

Solomon said,

> "Above all else, guard your heart, for everything you do flows from it."
>
> Proverbs 4:23

When you are good on the inside, you will be good on the outside.

During Jesus' time on the earth, the religious leaders made a big deal

---

165. *Romans 8:29-30*
166. *Luke 6:43-45*

out of what was seen. Washed hands, clean cups, and they would fast, pray and give so everyone could see them.

But Jesus said,

"Don't you see that whatever enters the mouth goes into the stomach and then out of the body? But the things that come out of a person's mouth come from the heart, and these defile them.

For out of the heart come evil thoughts - murder, adultery, sexual immorality, theft, false testimony, slander. These are what defile a person; but eating with unwashed hands does not defile them."[167]

People may say, there's something different about you. That's the "Lag" Indicator.

If you are consistent in putting the **Keys to Freedom** into practice, you should be seeing some good fruit in your life. Old mindsets start to change, and you will begin to live a different life. You are changing the way you think and in turn the way you act.

What's your fruit smell like?

I use "Fruit Tests" when I meet with someone to determine how to help them. Recently, I met with a man who told me he was struggling with anger. He said that since he became a Christian three years ago, he's gotten worse. The more he focuses on his anger issue the angrier he gets. I told him that's the problem. When you focus on Jesus and become like him, the anger issue will fade. When you focus on your "sin", you continue to struggle.

> "But the fruit of the Spirit is love, joy, peace,
> forbearance, kindness, goodness, faithfulness, gentleness
> and self-control. Against such things there is no law."
>
> Galatians 5:22-23

---

167. *Matthew 15:17-20*

I also use this when meeting with someone in conflict. Pastorally, if we must call someone in to meet with us over an issue, our goal is to work everything out for the best. The goal is to keep unity in the church. The person's response is totally up to them. We present what we've heard and they usually either respond in pride or humility. I am not responsible for their reaction. How they react will totally determine the next steps we take in moving forward.

If someone is struggling in their personal journey, I will usually ask, "how's your devotional life?" The answer to this question is always the same. "I've really let it go lately" or "I haven't been able to make time for it". The answer to any issue you are going through is always "Jesus".

I met with a longtime friend and Christian who was brave enough to meet with me about some behaviors he had done that he was ashamed of. It takes courage to confess your hidden bad behaviors to someone else. I didn't judge him but asked him if he was spending any time with God. He said truthfully, I haven't been doing that consistently over the past year. I told him what I'm telling you, the answer is easy, start right now or tomorrow morning spending time with him. Open your bible or devotional time. Pray. Spend time with Him.

Sniff test

Our fruit is a "Lag Indicator" of our spiritual progress. As we grow, our fruit should smell better and better. For instance, we should display more love in our lives.

As you consider the Fruit of the Spirit versus the Acts of the Flesh, how does your behavior smell? Do you pass the sniff test?

A sniff test or self-assessment is an informal check to determine if your fruit smells good or bad. How do you smell right now?

Fruit of the Spirit	Acts of the Flesh
Love	Sexual immorality
Joy	Impurity
Peace	Debauchery
Patience	Idolatry and witchcraft
Kindness	Hatred, discord, jealousy, fits of rage
Goodness	Selfish ambition
Faithfulness	Envy
Gentleness	Drunkenness
Self-Control	Orgies

Romans 12 is another great indicator of your fruit. How well do you stand up to this Christian standard?

We started off with lead indicators like renewing our minds. Then the lag indicator of testing and approving His perfect will should be taking place.

"Therefore, I urge you, brothers and sisters, in view of God's mercy, to offer your bodies as a living sacrifice, holy and pleasing to God—this is your true and proper worship. Do not conform to the pattern of this world but be transformed by the renewing of your mind. Then you will be able to test and approve what God's will is—his good, pleasing and perfect will."[168]

---

168. *Romans 12:1-2*

Then Romans 12:3-21 continues with, "For by the grace given me I say to every one of you: Do not think of yourself more highly than you ought, but rather think of yourself with sober judgment, in accordance with the faith God has distributed to each of you. For just as each of us has one body with many members, and these members do not all have the same function, so in Christ we, though many, form one body, and each member belongs to all the others.

We have different gifts, according to the grace given to each of us. If your gift is prophesying, then prophesy in accordance with your faith; if it is serving, then serve; if it is teaching, then teach; if it is to encourage, then give encouragement; if it is giving, then give generously; if it is to lead, do it diligently; if it is to show mercy, do it cheerfully."

- Love must be sincere.
- Hate what is evil; cling to what is good.
- Be devoted to one another in love.
- Honor one another above yourselves.
- Never be lacking in zeal, but keep your spiritual fervor, serving the Lord.
- Be joyful in hope, patient in affliction, faithful in prayer.
- Share with the Lord's people who are in need.
- Practice hospitality.
- Bless those who persecute you; bless and do not curse.
- Rejoice with those who rejoice; mourn with those who mourn.
- Live in harmony with one another.
- Do not be proud but be willing to associate with people of low position. Do not be conceited.
- Do not repay anyone evil for evil. Be careful to do what is right in the eyes of everyone.
- If it is possible, as far as it depends on you, live at peace with everyone.
- Do not take revenge, my dear friends, but leave room for God's

wrath, for it is written: "It is mine to avenge; I will repay," says the Lord.

On the contrary:

"If your enemy is hungry, feed him.
If he is thirsty, give him something to drink.
In doing this, you will heap burning coals on his head.
Do not be overcome by evil but overcome evil with good."

Back at the beginning of this book, we started with **Trusting the Process**.

A mature believer has the perspective that everything works together for our good. You must know that when you are a believer in Christ and seek after God that He is getting you to a place of Christ likeness.

So how do you know if you are growing in maturity?

Here are some good Indicators:

1. Worshipping God

The Mature Christian worships God in everything they do. Their very lives are an act of worship

"In everything they do, they do it with God in mind and to give God the glory."[169]

Their very life is so saturated with the presence of God that their lives shine with God's glory

When Moses went up on the mountain and spent time with God his face would glow. Spending time with God changes you. That's why your devotional time is not just a lead indicator but a lag indicator too. We never get away from worshiping God by spending time with Him.

True worship is not just worshiping God on Sunday before the sermon.

---

169. Colossians 3:23

It is helping the least of these. Widow and orphans. And visiting people in prison.

As we seek first God's Kingdom, He promises to give us everything we need. The amazing truth is that as we become more mature, what we desire becomes different.

> "Delight yourself also in the LORD, And He shall give you the desires of your heart."
>
> Psalm 37:4

N. T. Wright says, "You become like what you worship. When you gaze in awe, admiration, and wonder at something or someone, you begin to take on something of the character of the object of your worship."

Does your life worship God? Is it a reflection of Him? Does your light shine brightly to the world? Have the desires of your heart changed? Have your motives changed? Is spending time with God a priority?

2. Knowing Jesus
The Mature Christian demonstrates a passion to know, love and become like Jesus

"What is more, I consider everything a loss because of the surpassing worth of knowing Christ Jesus my Lord, for whose sake I have lost all things. I consider them garbage, that I may gain Christ and be found in him, not having a righteousness of my own that comes from the law, but that which is through faith in Christ – the righteousness that comes from God based on faith. I want to know Christ – yes, to know the power of his resurrection and participation in his sufferings, becoming like him in his death."[170]

As we get to know Jesus, we are transformed into His likeness. That's His desire for us.

---

170. *Philippians 3:8-10*

Do you look like Jesus? If not, what do you need to do to become more like Him?

3. The Word of God as a lifestyle
The Mature Christian knows and discerns God's Word and lives life based on the scriptures

One time, there was a longtime volunteer and leader who started acting contrary to our values and was negatively influencing his volunteers. I went to church leadership with the situation, and the leader said he wanted to pray about it.

Later he called me and said, "I have been searching the scriptures and 1 Timothy 5:1 says, "Do not rebuke an older man harshly, but exhort him as if he were your father". He went on to say I want to handle this carefully and with respect. He met with the man and gently talked with him. Soon after the man stepped down, but I was impacted by the way this leader handled the situation through the Word of God.

Do you consider the word of God in your decisions? Are you slow to react and take time to carefully consider the consequences? Is the Word of God your rule of conduct or is it an exception to the rule?

4. Unconditional love
A Mature Christian lives a life of love and displays unconditional love towards God, self and others

Ed Cole[171] said, "Love desires to give while lust desires to get". God's love is unselfish while the world's desires are selfish by nature.

I recently had the honor of walking my daughter, Bianca, down the aisle and give her in marriage to Ethan. It was such a moving moment for me. Later during the daddy daughter dance, I couldn't stop crying. There was something about the lyrics and holding her that made me so emotional.

---

171. *Edwin Louis Cole, Maximized Manhood, 1982*

I would love to keep my little girl forever. But that's selfish and not unconditional love. I gave my daughter away and gained a son-in-law and look forward to spoiling my grandchildren.

I also was blessed to officiate the wedding. Like most weddings, they wanted me to share 1 Corinthians 13 where the Apostle Paul defines what God's love looks like.

"Love is patient, love is kind. It does not envy, it does not boast, it is not proud. It does not dishonor others, it is not self-seeking, it is not easily angered, it keeps no record of wrongs. Love does not delight in evil but rejoices with the truth. It always protects, always trusts, always hopes, always perseveres.

Love never fails."

How well are you loving others without conditions? Would you say you are selfish or unselfish in your relationships?

5. The Fruit of the Spirit

A Mature Christian displays good fruit in his or her life. He/She is obedient to what Jesus commands us to do

Jesus said, "I am the true vine, and my Father is the gardener. He cuts off every branch in me that bears no fruit, while every branch that does bear fruit he prunes so that it will be even more fruitful."[172]

In Verse 8, He continues, "This is to my Father's glory, that you bear much fruit, showing yourselves to be my disciples."

We have to stay connected to Jesus to be fruitful. I didn't push obedience in the beginning because as we become like Jesus it is a natural output.

The Fruit of the Spirit includes self-control. A spiritually mature Christian holds his or her tongue. They have self-control over their "feelings". They are unselfish in dealing with others.

---

172. John 15:1-2

The Mature Christian is consistent and not washed up and down with their emotions. They are the same at home, work and church.

Jesus said to pray, fast and give in secret. A Mature Christian has the self-control and spiritual understanding to know that what they do in private is more important than doing it for show. God will reveal it in public.

How's your fruit smell? Do you see growth in your spiritual fruit?

6. Hard to offend
The Mature Christian is hard to offend and keeps the peace when possible

> "If it is possible, as far as it depends on you, live at peace with everyone."
> Romans 12:18

When you take a position of being hard to offend, it changes everything. Instead of taking offense, you view the other person as someone in need of your love. John Maxwell[173] says, "Hurting people hurt people". If you are in a healthy position, then you know the issue or misunderstanding is with the other person, you can take a proactive stance.

I share this often because people will leave the church over an offense. Never let someone chase you from your destiny. You can't stop them from saying negative or hurtful words, but you can control how you react to it.

Paul shared in Ephesians 4,

"So Christ himself gave the apostles, the prophets, the evangelists, the pastors and teachers, to equip his people for works of service, so that the body of Christ may be built up until we all reach unity in the faith and in the knowledge of the Son of God and become mature, attaining to the whole measure of the fullness of Christ."

---

173. John Maxwell, Winning with people, 2004

He goes on to share what our response will be as we become mature. "So that we may no longer be children, tossed to and fro by the waves and carried about by every wind of doctrine, by human cunning, by craftiness in deceitful schemes."[174]

How easy are you to offend? How quick are you to forgive and let things go? Do you hold a grudge?

7. Stewardship
The Mature Christian is generous with their time, talents and treasure and understands they are owners of nothing but stewards of everything

Do you know why you tithe? Did you know tithing is a form of maturity? Does generosity flow from you or do you hold things tightly?

One of the signs of maturity is that we tithe and give unselfishly to others. It's a matter of the heart. It can be hard at first to give 10% of your income if you have the wrong perspective.

I struggled with this for years until my now ex-wife left me, and I wasn't sure how I was going to make it. I went from two incomes to one overnight and still had a mortgage to pay. I couldn't afford not to tithe because I didn't know how I was going to keep the house. It wasn't even a matter of just giving God the leftovers. There were no leftovers.

It didn't happen overnight, but in 2008 there was a hurricane that hit Houston. It damaged my home, and I was without electricity for eleven days. I managed the insurance money and made sure all the projects were done well. I received a new roof, fence, some siding and paint job. I've never heard of this happening to anyone else but one day I received a check in the mail from my insurance company for $2500. It said it was for project management. I didn't ask for it, but it totally helped me out during that trying time.

---

174. Ephesians 4:14

A few years later, I was able to pay off my house and car and I was even able to put both my children through private school.

God says, to test Him. He will open the windows of heaven and pour out a blessing you can't even contain. He goes on to say that he will even defeat the enemy for your sake. When you tithe, you are even putting a hedge of protection around your family. Who knows what all He is protecting you from?[175]

When people ask about tithing, I like to share about Abraham. You see Abraham tithed ten percent of all the spoils he received during a big battle they won. He honored God with his wealth. He knew the first ten percent was God's. He did it from his heart.

This was centuries before the law came and required them to tithe. Now that Jesus has set us free from the curse of the law, we obey him from our hearts.

Just like Abraham, we need to give with the right motives. We do it because of our relationship with Him. As you grow in Christ and become more like Him you want to tithe because your heart has changed, and you are doing it out of this renewed heart.

Paul said, "Each person should do as he has decided in his heart–not reluctantly or out of necessity, for God loves a cheerful giver."[176]

We should give that same generosity to others when it comes to our time, talents, and treasure.

Spiritually mature Christians look for ways to be good to others. They have an unselfish desire to help people around them and people in need.

I am always thankful for men who have construction skills and help me go help others. Robert and Lindsey moved from Wisconsin to Houston to be at Lakewood Church. Robert is a contractor and he and his son Michael have helped us build a church at the Texas-Mexico border and

---

175. Malachi 3:10-11
176. 2 Corinthians 9:7

many other people in need after storms. Robert gives his time and his talents to help others.

How can you help others using the gifts God has given you?

8. Community

A Mature Christian understands the importance of unity in the church and the oneness of the Body of Christ

"And let us consider how we may spur one another on toward love and good deeds, not giving up meeting together, as some are in the habit of doing, but

encouraging one another—and all the more as you see the Day approaching."[177]

What was the one thing Jesus prayed for "ALL" believers? That we are one. Do you fight for unity or fight to be right?

Did you know Jesus prayed for you over 2,000 years ago?

> "My prayer is not for them alone. I pray also for those who will believe in me through their message, that all of them may be one, Father, just as you are in me and I am in you. May they also be in us so that the world may believe that you have sent me. I have given them the glory that you gave me, that they may be one as we are one — I in them and you in me — so that they may be brought to complete unity. Then the world will know that you sent me and have loved them even as you have loved me".
>
> John 17:20-23

---

177. Hebrews 7:9

A mature disciple knows how important it is to keep church unity. Sometimes that means letting an offense go or to not have to be right in a situation. Maybe you don't argue with someone even though you think you are right or ask forgiveness because of the way you reacted. Whatever the case, Jesus' prayer for us as believers today was that we would be one.

As we grow to become more like Him, we become more united. Our motives, personal agenda, and desires line up with His will.

The Holy Spirit is working in all believers to bring us to perfect unity. That's why you may hear several pastors teaching similar messages around the same time. Or why it seems like the pastor is speaking directly to you like he knows what you are going through. That's the Holy Spirit at work in all believers to bring us to oneness.

Planted in the House of the Lord

> "The righteous will flourish like a palm tree, they will grow like a cedar of Lebanon; planted in the house of the Lord, they will flourish in the courts of our God. They will still bear fruit in old age, they will stay fresh and green, proclaiming, 'The Lord is upright; He is my Rock, and there is no wickedness in Him.'"
> Psalm 92:12-15

Are you planted in the house of the Lord? Are you actively connected to a church community? Do you have the right mindset when it comes to unity and serving?

The promise is clear – when we are planted, we flourish. A palm tree bends in the storm but does not break. A cedar stands tall and strong. This is what happens when we remain firmly rooted in God's house.

You are a vital part of the body

God designed the Church to function as one body, with each person playing a unique and essential role:

> "Just as a body, though one, has many parts, but all its many parts form one body, so it is with Christ ... Now you are the body of Christ, and each one of you is a part of it."
>
> 1 Corinthians 12:12, 27

You were created to belong. No one is meant to do life alone. Whether you feel like a strong cedar or a struggling seedling, you are needed in the body of Christ. Your gifts, presence, and service make a difference!

The "get planted" challenge

I want to challenge you to take an intentional step toward being deeply rooted in God's house.

Here's how:

- **Find a Bible-based church** – one that preaches truth and fosters community.
- **Commit to faithfully attending and serving** – not just as a visitor but as a vital part of the family.
- **Bring your family and loved ones** – help them get involved, too.
- **Give us the next year of your life and it will never be the same for the better!** – watch how God moves in your life.

> "Let us not neglect meeting together, as some have made a habit, but let us encourage one another..."
>
> Hebrews 10:25

When you plant yourself in the house of God, your life becomes stronger, your purpose becomes clearer, and your faith grows deeper.

Will you take the challenge?

There is power in agreement

When you can let things go and lay aside differences and reach agreement, there is power.

The devil comes to kill to steal and to destroy but Jesus came to give you life and give it to the fullest. Where there are divisions, that's not from God.

One of the things we teach in Maximized Manhood is that we only do two things in life, enter and leave. How you leave something determines how you enter.

I always tell the guys to leave with a blessing. When you leave something hurt and offended, you are going to take that baggage with you. Leave with a blessing!

Your response says everything

How you respond to things reflects what's inside of you. Because of what God did for us through Jesus Christ, our response is to obey Him. Our perspective has changed. We no longer view things from a purely human point of view.

Because of what He did for you and me, we can now respond differently.

Under cover boss

> "How good and pleasant it is when God's people live together in unity! It is like precious oil poured on the head, running down on the beard, running down on Aaron's beard, down on the collar of his robe. It is as if the dew of Hermon were falling on Mount Zion.

For there the LORD bestows his blessing, even life forevermore."[178]

Like with Aaron, when we stay under the covering of God's authority, that blessing flows over us. I am faithful to remain under Joel Osteen's covering because as my pastor, he is receiving God's blessings and favor.

As I serve in ministry and align with the pastor's vision, that same blessing and favor is flowing over my life and the life of my family.

Gods got you covered! As you serve faithfully doing your best, God's blessing will flow over you and your entire family.

The scorecard

One thing is certain in life. One day we will pass away from this physical life. But that doesn't mean we cease to exist.

As Christians, we believe Jesus will return. In that moment, those of us who have fallen asleep (Died) and those who are currently alive will be transformed into the Image of Christ. We will receive a glorified body that will never decay.

The Bible also says, God will separate the wheat from the chaff. That is similar to the maintenance we do in our garden. We pick out the weeds and throw them away. He will separate out those who are In Christ from those who are not.

If you are a believer in Christ, your sins have been washed away. You won't have to face judgment. Jesus already redeemed you. But he will ask you what you did with his son, Jesus?

What's most important? That we believe and confess that Jesus is Lord. The scorecard is more of an indicator of how we are doing as we seek to grow and become more like Jesus.

---

178. Psalm 133

The end of the story

I don't know what you were told, but going to heaven when we die is not the end game.

Jesus promises a new heaven and a new earth. We will get a new glorified body and reign and rule with him in righteousness. Now that's good news!

What are you doing with what God gave you?

Jesus told a story about men with various talents. To one he gave one, to another he gave two, and still another he gave five. The story goes that a master of the men was expecting a return on his investment.[179]

We are stewards of the gifts God has given us. He is expecting us to do something with them.

It doesn't seem fair

When Tauren Wells[180] gets on stage and sings like an angel, then dances like Michael Jackson, and then preaches the word with passion and great communication, I am like a turtle hiding in my shell. God, why did you give him 100,000 talents and me just one?

But the important part of the story Jesus shared was what they did or didn't do with what God had given them. If you didn't use your talent, it was given to someone else who will. God expects us to be good stewards with what He gave us.

You may not think He hasn't given you much but that doesn't matter.

---

179. Matthew 25:14-30
180. Tauren Wells, Pastor, Church of Whitestone

The person with only one talent was afraid of using it so he buried it and when the master came back to check on his investment, he was disappointed. In fact, the master gave his one talent to Tauren Wells and now he has 100,001.

To the servants who invested their talents and got a return, the master said, well done my good and faithful servants.

While I'm partially joking about Tauren, the point is, don't waste your talents. Don't bury them or hide them from others. Step out in faith and use them to glorify God.

The promise is that one day you will hear Him say,

Well Done!

FREEDOM SCORECARD

Instructions:

Use the Freedom Scorecard on the next page to evaluate how you're doing with the lead and lag indicators.

Step 1: Give specific examples of your progress under each of the Lead Indicators.

Step 2: Rate each of the Lag Indicators. On a scale of 1 to

10, with 1 being the lowest level of progress or change and 10 being the highest. What are you doing well and where do you need to focus more attention?

Step 3: Go to the next steps on the following pages and write down your focus areas.

Suggestion: Complete a new *Freedom Growth Process Worksheet* based on where you are now.

Lifelong Learner: We never stop learning and growing. God wants to take you from glory to glory. Be a lifelong learner.

Freedom Scorecard
How's your freedom journey going? Rate your progress

Identity

Salvation

Identity in Jesus

Self-Awareness:
Know Who You Are

Owning Your Story

Let It Go

Forgiveness

Owning Your Story

Give examples of change in these areas. Where should you focus your attention?

Renewing Your Mind

Transformation

Watch Your Words

Devotional Life

Gratitude

Community

Testimony

Connection

Serving Others

Lead Indicators

Sniff Test
How's your fruit smell?

Worshipping God	☐	**Fruit of the Spirit**	☐	
Knowing Christ	☐	**Hard to Offend**	☐	
Word of God as a Lifestyle	☐	**Stewardship**	☐	
Display of Unconditional Love	☐	**Community**	☐	

Lag Indicators (Results)

on a Scale of 1 to 10 with 1 being lowest and 10 being highest

Appendix

Next Steps

Discover Your Design: Spiritual gifts self-assessment

The Freedom Growth Process worksheet

Memorization scriptures

Certificate of completion

Biography

WHAT'S NEXT?

Remember the **Freedom Growth Process**?

Ask someone you can trust to give you feedback on how you are doing. Does it line up with what you are thinking about yourself?

As you evaluate your fruit, is there an area you need to focus on next? Where do you feel like you are in your spiritual growth (Exploring Christ, Growing in Christ, Close to Christ, or Christ Centered)?

Remember, KNOWING CHRIST is our primary focus and meditation on scripture is the catalyst for growth at any level.

What's one thing you can focus on to grow in the right direction?

_____

_____

What steps can you take to move forward?

_____

_____

It is important to stay *Planted in the House of the Lord.* One of the best ways to maintain the progress you've made and continue to grow in spiritual maturity is to serve in your local church.

Where can you volunteer that aligns with your gifts, talents and abilities as well as what I've been through in life?

_____

_____

DISCOVER YOUR DESIGN

Spiritual Gifts Self-Assessment

Answer the following questions *(be as specific as you can in describing your response):*

1. What do you love to do?
(Example: I love to work with my hands. It energizes me when I build something, or I am naturally positive and love to encourage others.)
- I feel energized when I:
- I get excited when I think about doing:

2. What comes natural to you that you are good at doing?
(Example: I am good at organizing files and folders. I really like knowing where things are located.)
- I am naturally good at:

3. What gifts, talents or abilities do you have on your heart/desire to do more of in the future?
- I feel called to or my purpose in life is to:

What's Your Sweet Spot?

Use this Venn Diagram to reflect on where your passions, skills, and calling intersect:
- **What I Love**
- **What I'm Good At**
- **What I Feel Called To**

Spiritual Gifts Self-Assessment

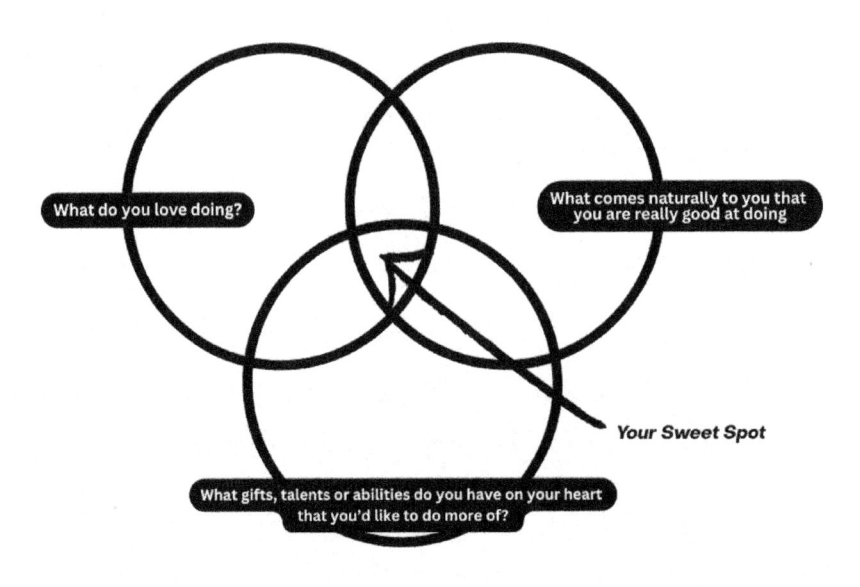

- What do you love doing?
- What comes naturally to you that you are really good at doing
- What gifts, talents or abilities do you have on your heart that you'd like to do more of?

Your Sweet Spot

The intersection is your Sweet Spot!
Purpose Statement: I was created to:

_____

Identify Your Top Spiritual Gifts

- Review the spiritual gifts and their descriptions list below.
- Based on your reflections, identify your top **three gifts** ranked in order of importance.
- Add them to the **Freedom Growth Process** Worksheet.

SPIRITUAL GIFTS SELF-ASSESSMENT TOOL

Instructions: Read each description and rate how true it feels for you using the scale below:

1. – **Rarely true**
2. – **Occasionally true**
3. – **Sometimes true**
4. – **Often true**
5. – **Consistently true**

Use your first instinct - don't overthink it! After rating, identify your strongest gifts.

Spiritual Gift	Description	Rating (1–5)
Wisdom	I often know the right thing to do in complex or confusing situations.	
Knowledge	I sense truth or insight that others may not see, often without prior learning.	
Discernment	I can sense when something isn't right spiritually or when someone is not genuine.	
Exhortation / Encouragement	I naturally lift people up and help them keep going.	
Faith	I trust God deeply even when things look impossible.	
Healing	I've prayed for or cared for someone and seen them healed.	
Miracles	I believe for and have witnessed God do the impossible through prayer.	
Discerning Spirits	I can sense the presence of good or evil spiritual influences.	

Spiritual Gift	Description	Rating (1–5)
Tongues	I speak or pray in a language I haven't learned, led by the Spirit.	
Interpreting Tongues	I can interpret spiritual language and make it understandable to others.	
Administration	I'm skilled at organizing people, projects, or systems efficiently.	
Leadership	People look to me for direction and I enjoy leading with vision and care.	
Apostleship	I enjoy starting new ministries or building up groups from the ground up.	
Evangelist	I naturally share the good news of Jesus and enjoy leading people to faith.	
Pastor / Shepherd	I care deeply for people and want to help them grow and stay spiritually healthy.	
Teaching	I love explaining biblical truths and helping others understand God's Word.	
Mercy	I feel deeply for those who are hurting and am drawn to help them.	
Service	I enjoy doing practical tasks that help others or the church.	
Helps	I like assisting others in their work and feel fulfilled in a support role.	
Prophecy	I often sense or speak what God is saying and feel called to share it boldly.	

NEXT STEPS

1. **Pray intentionally** this week and ask God to show you how to walk in your top gifts.
2. **Share your gifts** with a mentor or small group leader and ask for feedback.
3. **Find opportunities to serve** in your church, workplace, or community using your gifts.
4. **Keep a journal** to track how God confirms, grows, or redirects your gifts over time.
5. **Continue learning** about your gifts through Scripture, books, and conversations.
6. Add your top three Spiritual Gifts to the *Freedom Growth Process Worksheet*

> "Each of you should use whatever gift you have received to serve others, as faithful stewards of God's grace in its various forms."
>
> 1 Peter 4:10

FREEDOM GROWTH PROCESS WORKSHEET

1. Assessment
Take the Spiritual Gifts Self-Assessment
What Spiritual Gifts did you identify in your top three?

1.

2.

3.

How will I actively use one of my gifts in the next 30 days?

What training or mentoring could help me grow?

Who can I bless this week using this gift?

Ask one to three people who know you for honest, specific examples and feedback around what they have observed you doing well.

2. Personal Growth Plan

Based on your self-assessment, what would you like to do more of? What's your vision for your future self?

What steps can you take to move toward that vision?

1.

2.

3.

3. Development/Application

How are you going to put your steps into action? What development tools or applications are you going to apply?

Is there a volunteer opportunity at your church where you can grow in your gifting? For instance, if you have the gift of faith or healing, could you apply to be a prayer partner or in the hospital ministry?

4. Feedback

Who do you trust that you can ask for feedback on how you are progressing? Is there a Freedom Mentor or Life Coach who can walk with you on your journey?

Ask for honest feedback about your progress. Where have they seen positive progress? Ask for specific examples. Where do they think you have room for improvement or have seen any negative examples?

5. Progress/Repeat

How are you going to measure that you've achieved your growth plan?

What does success look like for you?

How can you use what you've learned to help someone else?

MEMORIZATION SCRIPTURES

Being confident of this, that he who began a good work in you will carry it on to completion until the day of Christ Jesus. Philippians 1:6	If you declare with your mouth, "Jesus is Lord," and believe in your heart that God raised him from the dead, you will be saved. Romans 10:9	Do not conform to the pattern of this world, but be transformed by the renewing of your mind. Then you will be able to test and approve what God's will is—his good, pleasing and perfect will. Romans 12:2
It is for freedom that Christ has set us free. Stand firm, then, and do not let yourselves be burdened again by a yoke of slavery. Galatians 5:1	And we know that in all things God works for the good of those who love him, who have been called according to his purpose. Romans 8:28	So if the Son sets you free, you will be free indeed. John 8:36
Do not be anxious about anything, but in every situation, by prayer and petition, with thanksgiving, present your requests to God. And the peace of God, which transcends all understanding, will guard your hearts and your minds in Christ Jesus. Philippians 4:6-7	For we know that our old self was crucified with him so that the body ruled by sin might be done away with, that we should no longer be slaves to sin— because anyone who has died has been set free from sin. Romans 6:6-7	By no means! We are those who have died to sin; how can we live in it any longer? Or don't you know that all of us who were baptized into Christ Jesus were baptized into his death? Romans 6:2-3

And God raised us up with Christ and seated us with him in the heavenly realms in Christ Jesus Ephesians 2:6	Therefore, if anyone is in Christ, the new creation has come: The old has gone, the new is here! 2 Corinthians 5:17	See what great love the Father has lavished on us, that we should be called children of God! And that is what we are! The reason the world does not know us is that it did not know him. 1 John 3:1
Through these he has given us his very great and precious promises, so that through them you may participate in the divine nature, having escaped the corruption in the world caused by evil desires. 2 Peter 1:4	So in Christ Jesus you are all children of God through faith, for all of you who were baptized into Christ have clothed yourselves with Christ. There is neither Jew nor Gentile, neither slave nor free, nor is there male and female, for you are all one in Christ Jesus. Galatians 3:26-28	For no matter how many promises God has made, they are "Yes" in Christ. And so through him the "Amen" is spoken by us to the glory of God. 2 Corinthians 1:20

Finally, brothers and sisters, whatever is true, whatever is noble, whatever is right, whatever is pure, whatever is lovely, whatever is admirable—if anything is excellent or praiseworthy—think about such things. Philippians 4:8	Consequently, faith comes from hearing the message, and the message is heard through the word about Christ. Romans 10:17	Now the Lord is the Spirit, and where the Spirit of the Lord is, there is freedom. And we all, who with unveiled faces contemplate the Lord's glory, are being transformed into his image with ever-increasing glory, which comes from the Lord, who is the Spirit. 2 Corinthians 3:17-18
Seek first the Kingdom of God and all His righteousness, and everything you need will be given unto you Matthew 6:33	Cast your cares on God because He cares for you. 1 Peter 5:7	Trust in the LORD with all your heart and lean not on your own understanding; in all your ways submit to him, and he will make your paths straight Proverbs 3:5-6
Rejoice always, pray continually, give thanks in all circumstances; for this is God's will for you in Christ Jesus. 1 Thessalonians 5:16-18	We demolish arguments and every pretension that sets itself up against the knowledge of God, and we take captive every thought to make it obedient to Christ. 2 Corinthians 10:5	I want to know Christ—yes, to know the power of his resurrection an*d participation in his sufferings, becoming like him in his death.* Philippians 3:10

For our struggle is not against flesh and blood, but against the rulers, against the authorities, against the powers of this dark world and against the spiritual forces of evil in the heavenly realms. Ephesians 6:12	They triumphed over him by the blood of the Lamb and by the word of their testimony; they did not love their lives so much as to shrink from death. Revelation 12:11	Submit yourselves, then, to God. Resist the devil, and he will flee from you. Come near to God and he will come near to you. Wash your hands, you sinners, and purify your hearts, you double-minded. James 4:7
Therefore, there is now no condemnation for those who are in Christ Jesus. Romans 8:1	"Come to me, all you who are weary and burdened, and I will give you rest. Take my yoke upon you and learn from me, for I am gentle and humble in heart, and you will find rest for your souls. For my yoke is easy and my burden is light." Matthew 11:28-30	The tongue has the power of life and death, and those who love it will eat its fruit. Proverbs 18:21

If God is for us, who can be against us? Romans 8:31	Now to him who is able to do immeasurably more than all we ask or imagine, according to his power that is at work within us, to him be glory in the church and in Christ Jesus throughout all generations, for ever and ever! Amen. Ephesians 3:20-21	I have learned the secret of being content in any and every situation, whether well fed or hungry, whether living in plenty or in want. I can do all this through him who gives me strength. Philippians 4:13
If it is possible, as far as it depends on you, live at peace with everyone. Romans 12:18	Delight yourself also in the LORD, And He shall give you the desires of your heart. Psalm 37:4	But the fruit of the Spirit is love, joy, peace, forbearance, kindness, goodness, faithfulness, gentleness and selfcontrol. Against such things there is no law. Galatians 5:22-23
If any of you lacks wisdom, you should ask God, who gives generously to all without finding fault, and it will be given to you. James 1:5	For it is by grace you have been saved, through faith— and this is not from yourselves, it is the gift of God — not by works, so that no one can boast. Ephesians 2:8-9	*My conscience is clear, but that does not vindicate me.* *It is the Lord who judges me.* *1 Corinthians 4:4*

Because you are his sons, God sent the Spirit of his Son into our hearts, the Spirit who calls out, *"Abba*, Father." Galatians 4:6	But you are a chosen people, a royal priesthood, a holy nation, God's special possession, that you may declare the praises of Him who called you out of darkness into his wonderful light. 1 Peter 2:9	For I know the plans I have for you," declares the Lord, "plans to prosper you and not to harm you, plans to give you hope and a future. Jeremiah 29:11
Brothers and sisters, I do not consider myself yet to have taken hold of it. But one thing I do: Forgetting what is behind and straining toward what is ahead Philippians 3:13	For if you forgive other people when they sin against you, your heavenly Father will also forgive you. Matthew 6:14	If you forgive anyone's sins, their sins are forgiven; if you do not forgive them, they are not forgiven. John 20:23
Therefore, since we are surrounded by such a great cloud of witnesses, let us throw off everything that hinders and the sin that so easily entangles. And let us run with perseverance the race marked out for us. Hebrews 12:1	This *is* the day the LORD has made; We will rejoice and be glad in it. Psalm 118:24	In the same way, let your light shine before others, that they may see your good deeds and glorify your Father in heaven. Matthew 5:16

So in everything, do to others what you would have them do to you, for this sums up the Law and the Prophets. Matthew 7:12	Do you not know that in a race all the runners run, but only one receives the prize? Run in such a way as to take the prize. 1 Corinthians 9:24	"In this world, you will have trouble. But take heart! I have overcome the world." John 16:33
"The thief comes only to steal and kill and destroy; I have come that they may have life and have it to the full." John 10:10	"So I say, walk by the Spirit, and you will not gratify the desires of the flesh. For the flesh desires what is contrary to the Spirit, and the Spirit what is contrary to the flesh. They are in conflict with each other, so that you are not to do whatever you want." Galatians 5:16-17	"At the name of Jesus every knee should bow, in heaven and on earth and under the earth, and every tongue acknowledge that Jesus Christ is Lord, to the glory of God the Father." Philippians 2:10-11

FREEDOM CERTIFICATE OF COMPLETION

I hereby acknowledge that I, _____, have completed

Your Freedom Journey milestones this _____ day of _____, 20____.

Your Freedom Journey Milestones:
- Prayer of Salvation / Rededication
- Re-labeled Exercise
- Daily Declarations
- Spiritual Gifts Self-Assessment
- Thoughts Inventory
- Scriptures Memorization
- Words Inventory
- Daily Devotional Time
- Gratitude List
- Setting Boundaries / In & Out of Bounds Exercise
- Forgiveness Letter
- Life Story
- Testimony
- Connection: Small Group Participation
- Serving Others: Volunteering

If you completed the milestones with a Freedom Life Coach or qualified Freedom Facilitator, what was their name?

_____

Signature of Participant: _____

YOUR FREEDOM JOURNEY

Completion Verification

Complete the online form

Congratulations on completing **Your Freedom Journey**.

Complete the online form to receive your official Certificate of Completion.

Online Form

FREE TO SOAR • 301

Free to Soar Post-Assessment

Unlock Your Potential Today

Scan the QR Code Below

freetosoarbook.com

YOUR FREEDOM JOURNEY CONTINUES...

If this book has positively impacted you, and you experienced life change, please share your story with me at:

freetosoarbook@gmail.com

Let's stay connected!

Here's my *LinkTree* for more ways to connect.

***Coming Soon*: Freedom Life Coaching**
Training and Certification

About the author

JOHN BOWMAN

John Bowman is a Senior Director and Pastor at Lakewood Church in Houston, Texas.

He has spent his life developing leaders and empowering volunteers. From swim coach in high school to developing leaders at one of the largest churches in America, John's passionate focus is bringing out the best in others.

He was the director of leadership and workforce development at a community college when he experienced a life altering change through his salvation and belief in Jesus as his Lord and Savior in late 2000.

Immediately after, he was recruited by Development Dimensions International (DDI) and helped global corporations with their talent management.

- He assisted a national healthcare organization in reducing their turnover from 29% to 19% saving the company hundreds of millions of dollars
- After a major oil spill, he orchestrated a team to change the safety culture of a global oil company

- He helped several global organizations to develop their succession plans and hi-potential leadership pools including the selection of the next CEO for a fortune 500 company

In January 2001, John and his family started attending Lakewood Church in Houston, Texas.

In 2011, John was ordained as a Pastor at Lakewood Church and became the director of the Men's Ministry.

In 2013, he was asked to also oversee the Lakewood Internship Program, Leadership Development Program, LifeGroups, Single's Ministry and Men's Ministry.

In 2017, he helped coordinate the response and recovery efforts to assist Lakewood members and volunteers following the deviation of Hurricane Harvey.

In 2018, he was asked to transition the church's programs assisting people experiencing life's struggles and addictions. Out of this transition birthed the Freedom Ministry.

He is the architect of Lakewood's Freedom Program and ***Your Freedom Journey*** which was designed as a yearlong curriculum to help people experience inner freedom and purpose. It is impacting thousands of lives each year from around the world to change for the better.

In 2024, he was asked to develop team leaders to respond proactively to help people in crisis recover following natural disasters.

Most recently, John was Board Certified through the American Association of Christian Counselors (AACC) programs for Life Coaching and Mental Health Coaching.

John is married to Laura and has two grown children, Brandon and Bianca.

Printed in Dunstable, United Kingdom